Nathan Yates covered the murders of Holly Wells and Jessica Chapman as a *Daily Mirror* staff reporter, from the day of the girls' disappearance to the trial of Ian Huntley and Maxine Carr at the Old Bailey. Days before their arrest, he interviewed Huntley and Carr and was invited into their home. He followed every twist of the huge police manhunt and witnessed first-hand the terrible ordeal of the Wells and Chapman families.

The in-depth reporting of these events won Nathan and his colleagues the title Team Reporters of the Year at the 2003 British Press Awards. Nathan has been at the *Daily Mirror* for six years and has worked for four other national newspapers since leaving Oxford University with a first-class degree in English.

D0581428

BEYOND
EVIL

NATHAN YATES

BEYOND
EVIL

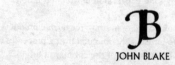

JOHN BLAKE

Published by John Blake Publishing Ltd,
3, Bramber Court, 2 Bramber Road,
London W14 9PB, England

www.blake.co.uk

First published in paperback in 2005

ISBN 1 84454 142 8

British Library Cataloguing-in-Publication Data:

A catalogue record for this book is available from the British Library.

Design by www.envydesign.co.uk

Printed and bound in Great Britain by Bookmarque Ltd

10

*The author wishes to thank Janice,
Colin and Ben Yates, Piers Morgan, Andy Lines and
Conor Hanna, Ian Vogler, Aidan McGurran, Lorraine
Fisher and others, without whom this book could
not have been written.*

CONTENTS

1

THE FIND

It was an everyday scene in the Suffolk countryside. A bright August sun shining on a land of low hillocks and copses, the trees heavy with the green leaves of late summer. At this isolated spot a mile and a half north of the nearest village, Lakenheath, there was little to disturb the silence apart from the occasional deep boom of a jet landing or taking off from the adjacent airbase. In the quiet earth track leading up to the twelve-foot-high wire fence shielding the military property, the only movement to be seen were the walking figures of local gamekeeper Keith Pryer and his friends Adrian Lawrence and Helen Sawyer, who were treading the bank of the roadway a few yards from a pheasant pen.

Keith had parked his four wheel drive Isuzu where the

1

track, called Common Drove, ran between two rows of beech trees and entered a wooded area known as The Carr. At this point, around 12.30pm on Saturday August 17 2002, the trio were wading through the overgrown verge 600 yards from where Common Drove joined the partially tarmacked road to the hamlet of Wangford. The trees, the sunshine, the sound of the 600 fledgling pheasants cheeping softly in the wood – there was nothing to suggest that the scene of pastoral peace was about to be ruptured by the most unimaginable horror. Nothing, that is, except for the strange, terrible smell which seemed to emanate from somewhere in the ditch.

Keith was used to the odours of the countryside, but there was something unusual about the pungent, sickening stench he had noticed in this area over the past few days. It was so distinctively unpleasant that he and his companions had decided to find out what was causing it. They thought perhaps a farmer had dumped manure in the woods, or maybe a dead sheep. In their darkest nightmares they could not have imagined the truth. Suddenly, Adrian, who was leading the party, gave a shout. He turned, his face white with shock, and yelled to his girlfriend: 'Don't come any further Helen – get back in the van.'

Keith approached and peered into the ditch. What happened next was to stay fixed in his memory, probably forever. Scanning the damp soil in the bottom of the five-foot-deep cutting, he could see there was a strange object lying there. For a split second, he could not make out what it was – then the shapes leaped into focus. He could make out the outline of what could only be a body. Covered in a

2

shallow coating of grime, it was a body so small and fragile it had to be that of a child. It was badly disfigured, blackened and burnt to the point where the tiny skeleton was showing through the charred remains of the flesh. And lying next to it was another, equally pitiful, equally blackened figure. They were barely recognisable as human. They had been placed carefully side by side. As police officers would later relate with revulsion and astonishment, it appeared as if whoever had put them there had taken meticulous pains to destroy them. Their flesh had been burnt to the point where they had become, in the words of pathologist Dr Nat Cary, 'partially skeletonised'.

The heartbreaking sight left Keith instantly sick, as if his stomach had turned inside out in a split second. Staggering in a state of confusion, he had no idea what to do or what to think. The 48-year-old gamekeeper is himself the father of two grown-up children, and he had been following the events in Soham, just across the county border in Cambridgeshire, with the fear and foreboding shared by much of the nation during this period of August 2002. This quiet, moustached figure is regarded as a capable character, not easily put off his stride. His work looking after game birds on a 4,000 acre estate made him familiar with the natural cycle of life and death, and he was not at all squeamish when it came to carrying out his job. But nothing in his experience looking after pheasants could have prepared him for this. Somehow he and Adrian managed to get back to the jeep and call the police.

To this day, the gamekeeper finds it disturbing to talk about the horror he witnessed. 'I wasn't prepared for what I saw,' he said. 'There were what appeared to be two very badly decomposed human bodies lying side by side. I noticed the smell of rotting flesh.'

According to Keith's friend, farmer Brian Rutterford who works the surrounding land, what Keith saw on that day was truly the stuff of nightmares. 'It was horrific,' said Brian, who rents the fields in this area from the well-known East Anglian landlords Elvedon Estates. 'Keith is a proper family man and this has really shaken him. I think it's worse if you've got kids of your own because you can imagine all too well what the parents are going through. I was one of the few people he managed to talk to just after he had found them and he told me exactly how he had found them, exactly what they looked like. Apparently they were very badly destroyed, so you couldn't tell straight away what they were. And whoever did it put them side by side in the ditch. It was horrible, not the sort of thing anyone would ever want to see. He was trembling all over, very, very shocked and scared.'

Keith would be reminded of his grisly discovery the next day and every day for months afterwards as he was forced to walk past the spot to continue feeding his birds. The walk would become a matter of endurance for him as he struggled to come to terms with what he had found, and each time he went past that place he would wish that he had not been in the group which made the discovery. But those details of analysis would come later. At that moment he retained just enough composure to realise what the rest of the world realised soon afterwards: that these were the remains of Holly Wells and Jessica Chapman, two healthy, happy young girls just 10 years old, who had vanished without trace 13 days ago from the town of Soham, in neighbouring Cambridgeshire.

Over the past fortnight, hundreds of police officers had been scouring the countryside for signs of the girls, digging up hedges, dredging rivers and carrying out door-to-door enquiries. Their parents, Kevin and Nicola Wells and Leslie and Sharon Chapman, had endured a living hell as everyone – local people, policemen, journalists and the public watching the television news or reading the papers – hoped against hope that the girls would be found alive. Since Holly and Jessica disappeared from the Wellses' home shortly after 5pm on Sunday, 4 August, the search for them had become a national event. In workplaces, pubs and cafés across the land people were talking about the missing schoolgirls and hoping they would be found safe and well. The two families had suffered a very public ordeal as the search went on; they staged a series of agonising press conferences, facing the cameras to speak of their torment in a desperate attempt to move an abductor to pity. Detectives struggled to piece together the minute detail of the girls' final movements but, of all the theories voiced by all the witnesses, few suggested the girls had been snatched by a 28-year-old caretaker whom they knew and trusted. Only hardened policemen and reporters thought there was something odd about Ian Huntley's part in the story.

Privately, there were many, including the parents, who

had a gut feeling from the beginning that this was a case of kidnapping. Experienced policemen and journalists at the scene knew it was unlikely the girls would ever be found alive. As the days ticked by, those uncomfortable private views came more and more to the forefront of people's minds. Yet still, just under a fortnight after Holly and Jessica had vanished, there was the temptation to hope against hope. When Keith Pryer found the bodies in the ditch, the hope shared by millions was finally demolished. All the theories had turned out to be wrong, all the searching had come to nothing. It was a sickening blow, and it is little wonder that the man who suffered it first-hand felt physically ill.

Thousands of people from all over the world had been sending in their messages of support for the families of Holly and Jessica. Soon they would be sending their messages of mourning instead, either by email or by letter or in the form of bunches of flowers. The bouquets would pile high in the grounds of St Andrew's Church in Soham, in scenes reminiscent of the public mourning for Princess Diana or the Queen Mother.

For Keith and Brian, as for others involved in this extraordinary case, its most puzzling and perhaps most disturbing feature was the senseless savagery of the murders, a savagery cloaked in a sick appearance of care. Someone had committed a double child murder, a crime which could hardly be surpassed in its gruesome and callous nature. Yet this same person had driven these girls to an idyllic spot in the countryside and laid them to rest side by side. It would later emerge that that someone had also posed as the girls' friend, almost like an older brother, and that his girlfriend, who helped conceal his guilt, was regarded as a kind of sister to them.

Those responsible were not paedophiles who snatched the girls from the street and bundled them into the back of a van, but a young man and woman who knew them and their families, who were well thought of in the local community. These were the disturbing paradoxes of a killer who acted as though he cared, of a caretaker who killed.

2

PORTRAIT OF A KILLER

The man responsible for this terrible act, Ian Huntley, was being held at a police station in Ely, Cambridgeshire, when Keith Pryer made his discovery. Huntley was trying to convince officers that he was a man so innocent the accusations against him were driving him mad. The 28-year-old caretaker was dribbling, foaming at the mouth and crying incessantly during questioning. He hardly spoke a word, and the sounds he did make were gibberish. From the moment he came under suspicion, Huntley denied all knowledge of the girls' disappearance, a façade of innocence which he kept up right through his initial court appearances. Under repeated questioning by officers both before and after his arrest, he continued to claim he had done nothing to hurt the girls.

The appearance of the man languishing in the cells

accused of murder betrayed nothing of his lethal nature. He was unremarkable to look at, of medium height and build, with close-cropped dark hair and skin which was also dark but without the healthy glow of a tan. It had an ashen tinge which could have been an indication of infrequent washing. A stubbly growth of beard grew in a patchy fashion at the bottom of his rounded cheeks and on the front of his chin. His unkempt appearance showed the dire straits in which the caretaker found himself. According to those close to him, he was normally very concerned about the way he looked, to the point of being vain. A former colleague from the Heinz factory in his home town of Grimsby remembers: 'He looked much smarter than the others, even at work. You never saw him wearing old tracksuits and stuff like that, it was always cord trousers and shirts. When he went out on a Saturday night he made a real effort. He saw himself as a ladies' man.' Huntley's habits were to bathe and shave every morning, clean his teeth twice a day and always keep his hair neatly cut, short but not spiky. His dirty-looking skin had nothing to do with lack of hygiene.

Several of Huntley's many conquests had thought him quite good-looking, in a bland way. The circular face held regular features, and his active life had kept him slim. But what distinguished him from others was less his facial landscape than a permanent look of distance, or even hurt, in his eyes. They were, according to one former girlfriend, the eyes of a wounded animal. 'At the beginning I thought he had sensitive eyes, but it was really more that he always looked like he felt sorry for himself,' the woman, now 26, said. 'The way he would look at me reminded me of a deer or a cow. But when he was mad about something or he wanted to tell me what to do, they were different. He could change completely, so he was really glaring at me. It was scary.'

Since Huntley's arrest, many have remarked that this split personality was captured in one telling photograph which shows the killer posing in the grounds of Soham Village College. Huntley looks straight into the camera, with an expression which at first sight appears sad and concerned. But detectives noticed a strange quality about the picture. One explained: 'If you cover the right side of it with your hand and look into his right eye he's got a look of being sorry for himself. If you cover the left side of the photo and look into his left eye, there's this expression of absolute cruelty. The first time I did this, the effect was so striking it made me jump.'

After murdering Holly and Jessica 13 days earlier, Huntley's eyes had become rimmed by deep black shadows, a sign, perhaps, that he hadn't been getting much sleep. He had lost weight, not more than a few pounds but enough from his already quite spare frame to make his trousers loose around his waist. According to his own version of events, he was being driven headlong towards a breakdown by continual police harassment. This treatment was particularly difficult to deal with, he would explain in letters sent from his cell, for a character like his. For, in his own mind, Huntley was a sensitive soul who found it difficult to cope with emotional turmoil. And certainly he was sensitive to his own pain, though much less so to the pain of others. During his life before killing Holly and Jessica, he had tried to do away with himself three times. As he sat in his temporary cell on Saturday, 17 August, there was little doubt that the pressure was beginning to tell.

With the ongoing burden of lying about his actions and hiding the truth, he was getting worn down, and it showed in his behaviour with police. When he was first questioned before his arrest, his responses had been expansive, his sympathies for the girls strongly uttered. But, after he was arrested, he had refused to say more than the bare minimum. With time he had become more and more morose and withdrawn. As we shall see, such moods were part of Huntley's personality, but there was no doubt that he was sinking now. He spoke much less often, replying increasingly in monosyllables or not at all. He was spending all of his time locked away entirely by himself.

According to Huntley, one thing which tortured him was imagining the grief of the Wells and Chapman families. Earlier, during his many conversations with journalists, he had expressed his torment over a disappearance which, he said, 'beggared belief'. He had watched with a face contorted in sympathy as the families had given a string of emotional press conferences in front of TV cameras, pleading for the return of their children. At this moment in the cells, there is every reason to suppose that he continued to think of these people – without ever admitting he had destroyed their lives.

Later, when police told him the bodies had been found, he would be racked with fear that the detectives were about to discover some incriminating clue. He would also think again of Kevin and Nicola Wells and Leslie and Sharon Chapman and their ordeal. Not only had Huntley known these people almost as neighbours in the small town of Soham, and as parents of children he worked with every day, he also had spent many hours with them during the hunt for the missing girls. As they begged for the abductor to return their children in the assembly hall of Soham Village College, the killer was for much of the time standing only a few feet away.

Much has been written about how the deaths of Holly and Jessica caused unspeakable grief to their parents, and it seems callous to entertain the idea that Huntley himself may have been stricken by guilt. In none of his statements under questioning did he say he was sorry, and he consistently refused to accept responsibility for what he had done. Yet the constant denials could reveal a mind which could not come to terms with the reality of its actions. Before he was unmasked as the killer, Huntley said he imagined what it was like going through the agony of the girls' parents and pondered the ordeals of the girls themselves. We shall never know for certain how much truth there was in these claims and to what extent they were purely an attempt to put on a face of innocence. He pretended to be, like the rest of the world, wondering how this tragedy came to pass. Yet he was the murderer and could run through the acts from memory. It is possible that Huntley's bafflement over the crime may have been partly genuine. He may have been tortured by the question: why had he murdered these two innocent girls and left so many lives in ruins? Sitting on his own in his cell, he may well have pondered these issues. Over the course of his coming life sentence, he would have plenty of time to reflect.

Doctors who studied Huntley at Rampton Hospital would diagnose him as a psychopath. By this they meant that he was capable of committing crimes without experiencing a normal person's feelings of regret. In their view, Huntley had a personality disorder which made him immune to society's moral code.

Whether Huntley did or did not feel guilt, police and psychiatrists who came into contact with him say there is strong evidence of self-hatred in his character. Since childhood he had experienced huge mood swings. He had described how at times he felt confident, arrogant and better than anyone else around him. He would bolster his self-esteem by a series of pretences designed to make him the subject of others' admiration. Yet, away from the fantasies, at other times he experienced severe depression, feeling inadequate and rejected, particularly by women. At this, the lowest point in his life, these deep inadequacies were no doubt playing through his consciousness with a renewed force. Now he was one of the most despised people on the planet – even other criminals would hate him and be after his blood.

Always obsessed with getting away with his crimes, Huntley had dreaded capture. He had derived a sense of superiority from deceiving others, and during the murder hunt he had revelled in acting out his innocence. His deceptions had been a tool to control others; he had used his lies to manipulate people from early childhood, for power over others was something he always craved. Now his deception had been demolished; he was left naked without his mask, and utterly under the control of forces far more powerful than himself. He had reached rock bottom.

In a similar cell 30 miles away at Peterborough police station, Huntley's girlfriend, Maxine Carr, was also in a state of torment. A 25-year-old woman of average looks and greasy appearance, she was so disturbed that she found it impossible to eat and she was losing weight rapidly. Huntley had meant the world to her, and despite his arrest she was still hopelessly bound to him. He was the first man who had wanted to stay with her, and she had invested everything in him. For Carr, Huntley offered the hope of a future with a man she loved; she had been prepared to stand by him through anything in the belief that they would be together for ever and would have a family. Sitting in her cell, she remained utterly emotionally dependent on the man who had landed her there, and talked about Huntley constantly, begging police for news of him. His dominating behaviour, which had driven away many other women, had been for her a sign of the devotion she so desperately needed.

Before Huntley had murdered the girls, Carr had felt she was at the beginning of a better life. Settled in a relationship at last, she had moved with her man to a new area of the country and both had managed to get better jobs than they had had before. Now, all that had been completely destroyed. She had lost her future husband, her home and her life. Carr had hoped for so much from her relationship with this man. How could she, how could they, end up like this? Did the secret lie somewhere in their past?

3

A TURBULENT LIFE

Ian Kevin Huntley was born into a life of instability, uncertainty and poverty, and from early childhood his existence was turbulent. When he came into the world, on 31 January 1974 at Grimsby Maternity Hospital, his parents, Kevin and Lynda, were already struggling to get by on pittance wages. His father worked as a gas fitter and the family saved money by lodging with Lynda's parents at 100 Wintringham Road in Grimsby. The couple had married when they realised Lynda was three months pregnant with their first child. Both were only 18 when they signed the wedding papers on 23 June 1973, and at that point Kevin Huntley was just an apprentice in his chosen trade, while Lynda Huntley held down a poorly paid job in a printing works. With little income and no place of their own, the young couple would struggle to support their newborn child. Kevin would have to work overtime while his wife gave up her job to look after the baby.

Soon the hard work paid off and the family were able to move into their own home, a rented house at 1 Pelhams Road, Immingham, a few miles north of Grimsby. However, their task was made still harder when, on 16 August 1975, the birth of Huntley's younger brother, Wayne, completed the family. Kevin Huntley found himself weighed down with the responsibility of a wife and two children. Tired and overworked, he was a dour father, strict with his family. Friends remember him as an unsmiling individual, dark and pinched, with a stern aspect, mature for his age. He took his trade very seriously and was a good worker. Despite his dour appearance he was devoted to his wife and would do anything to look after her.

The infant Huntley was also devoted to his mother, and became intensely jealous when this bond was challenged by Wayne's arrival. With less than two years between the brothers, Lynda's maternal attentions had to be divided. Huntley reacted to this with jealous furies so uncontrollable that they astonished his parents and their friends. Already his solution was to manipulate; placed in a situation he hated, he hit back by cheating his way to the attention he lacked. He would frequently deceive Lynda into caring for him and ignoring Wayne by bursting into tears at the slightest provocation. On many occasions he kept both parents up all night. A friend of the family remembers: 'Ian was a handful as a baby. He was always screaming and crying and wanting his mum. He seemed to do it a lot when she was bothering with the younger one, as if he couldn't stand her giving attention to Wayne.' This jealousy of his brother was to be a driving force in Huntley's life, and he would continue to be possessed by it almost 30 years later. Huntley's former wife, Claire Evans, is among many who believe the envy has marred his whole life.

Another family circumstance which seems to have had a huge impact on him was his father's sternness. Kevin Huntley's strict code of behaviour seems to have made a strong impression on the youngster, and he grew up distant from his father, becoming something of a mummy's boy and taking Lynda's side in any argument. A friend of the family said: 'As far as Ian was concerned, Lynda was always in the right and Kevin was always in the wrong. If there were any problems in the family, Ian blamed his father for them.' The Huntley home during these early years was in a solidly working-class district. Immingham is a town at the mouth of the Humber estuary, and many of its inhabitants are employed in shipping or related industries. In the 1970s the way of life was unchanged in essentials from Victorian days, when the area's first fish-processing plants and industrialised fishing fleet were established.

Huntley would later become one of Immingham's many manual labourers, but for the time being his surroundings were restricted at first to the family home and then extended to include the town's Eastfield Junior School, which he attended from the age of five. Although Huntley was later to make defenceless schoolgirls his own victims, back then he was the one who was the target of abuse.

From the moment he walked into the school, classmates regarded him as the first choice if they wanted to hit someone or dish out verbal cruelties. 'He was the class loner really. If anyone was ever bullied, it was him,' recalled Matt Walker, 28, an assistant manager of an industrial supplier who had known Huntley since they were both five years old. Huntley's large pale forehead got him the cruel nickname of 'The White Cliffs of Dover'. Children would also call him 'Spadehead' because of the strange square shape of his face. Huntley, a sickly child who suffered from asthma, was in no position to defend himself against bullying. Matt remembers him trying to bluff his way through this kind of hostility, obviously having no idea of how to deal with it properly. He added: 'He was the kind of kid who would give a lot of mouth to people, but if they turned on him he would go running to the teacher.'

Huntley's tale-telling made him even more of a hate figure with the other pupils and his attempts to make friends were disasters. In a foretaste of his later life of fantasy, he would even make up tittle-tattle to spread as much disruption as possible. Another former pupil at Eastfield said: 'Everyone hated him. He caused so much trouble making stories up about people who didn't like him, and that turned out to be pretty much everyone. The teachers didn't like him much either.' The result of Huntley's bizarre behaviour was a total lack of close friends. Carl McLaughlin, another classmate, remembers, 'He used to get bullied really badly. He was a loner.' During this period, Huntley encountered another, still more serious form of abuse. He was beaten and sexually abused by an adult. He would later tell friends and acquaintances of this terrible experience. It was, he said, an ordeal which left him scarred for life.

At the age of 11 Huntley moved to Healing Comprehensive School, one of the better schools in the area and later attended by Maxine Carr. Here he proved to be equally unpopular, and classmates remember him as a 'scruffy outcast' who always wore a battered, fake-leather jacket and had no friends. One former pupil recalls how he had developed his habit of lying to teachers. He said: 'Huntley was terrible at football and the other kids would take the mickey out of him for it. So every time we were supposed to play football during a games lesson he would suddenly have a massive asthma attack. It's true that he did have asthma, but the funny thing was that it always seemed to come on much worse during football, and the attacks happened for example when he let a goal in or made some other cock-up. It was obvious he was faking it, but all the same the way he could do the cough and wheeze was just like it was for real. He was a very good actor, I'll give him that much.'

In the first form at Healing Huntley became the target of abuse from the older pupils. Fifth- and sixth-formers would frequently beat him up in the playground, and on one occasion he was found hanging by his jumper from a peg in the cloakroom, unable to get down. He was also subjected to a practice known as 'kegging', where two older boys would grab his legs and pull his groin into a post in the yard. The punishment seems savage, but classmates felt little pity for Huntley, insisting he deserved it for his devious habits. In the course of this ordeal his school work also suffered. Never the brightest of pupils, Huntley slid behind in key subjects like Maths and English.

After two years at Healing the situation had become so bad that Huntley moved school to Immingham Comprehensive, considered in the area to be a rougher, less middle-class institution. He arrived there at the beginning of the third form, the hope being that he could make a fresh start at an age when he was growing bigger and becoming less easy to victimise. Unfortunately, the escape did not work as well as planned. He again failed to make any friends and was bullied physically and verbally. Known here simply as 'Huntley', the nearest he came to any real contact with his fellow pupils was through a nerdish preoccupation with computer games. Former classmate Kevin Scott, 29, said: 'He was weak-minded and often bullied. I did have the misfortune of hanging around him. We swapped computer games – he was very average and not very popular. He seemed terrified of his dad, who, I think, was quite strict. Once he came round for tea and his plastic computer-game case got broken. He was petrified about what his dad would say.'

Desperate to make friends, Huntley joined the 2nd Immingham Scouts during his first term at his new school. But he left two months later because he couldn't stand the physical activities and remained unpopular with the others. Then, at the age of 13, he revealed what was to become a lifelong passion for aeroplanes by joining the Air Training Corps. The move was inspired partly by his father, who felt the military ethic would give his son some much-needed discipline, but Huntley grew to like the idea less for the training than for the machines themselves. He dreamt of joining the RAF, and would cling on to that vision for years to come, later boasting in pubs that he had been a pilot. Yet in the event he spent only one year with 866 Squadron – known as the 'Flying Vikings' – before leaving the cadets. From then on his contact with real aircraft would be restricted to watching them as he developed the hobby of plane spotting.

Another former classmate, Adrian Good, remembers the beginnings of this pastime. 'As a child, he was totally obsessed with aeroplanes,' he said. 'He would scribble down details and talk about them all the time.' Huntley's fantasy world of aeroplanes offered him an escape from teenage problems and insecurities; while dreaming of being a pilot he could imagine himself as a powerful, independent figure in charge of his own destiny. It could be argued that his other hobbies during this period, weightlifting and shooting air rifles, served similar purposes. Huntley liked to feel himself in command of a powerful machine or weapon, he wanted to be physically strong and possess a body which would impress others.

He would spend hours building models of his favourite aircraft, painting them and suspending them from his bedroom ceiling. He would also pore over plane-spotting magazines and put up posters of his favourite jets on the walls. One of these was the Harrier Jump Jet, which had seen much action during the 1983 Falklands War. Huntley remained so smitten with this plane that in his late twenties he would make pilgrimages to airbases to watch it in action. This was how he became familiar with the airbase at Lakenheath and the land around it, where one day the bodies of Holly Wells and Jessica Chapman would be discovered.

Back at Immingham Comprehensive, the hostility of his schoolmates and the disappointment caused by his failures with the Scouts and the Air Training Corps were getting to Huntley. He became so desperate for attention that he attempted suicide in what would be the first of at least three such efforts. He stole a box of paracetamol painkillers from his mother's medicine cabinet and swallowed the lot while his parents were out. Friends say Lynda found him lying on his bed barely conscious, and he was taken by ambulance to Grimsby Hospital for an urgent stomach pump. Huntley's life may well have been in danger if his mother had not returned in time, but the bid to take his life did not inspire sympathy at school. One classmate said: 'He did it because he wanted people's attention, it was as simple as that. I don't believe for a minute he really wanted to die, it was just a stunt to get people to notice him and feel sorry for him. It was just an act he pulled because he didn't have any friends.' Ex-pupils of Immingham have a similar attitude to Huntley's asthma attacks. Another said: 'He would take massive puffs of his inhaler so everyone would think he was really sick, but we mostly didn't believe him because it was Huntley and we all knew he was a liar. He couldn't bear people not to notice him all the time and he wanted everyone to think he was marvellous. The problem was we all thought he was a prat.'

Some believe the trigger for Huntley's first suicide attempt was his being rejected by one of the girls in his class. This is quite possible given his precocious sexual behaviour. For from an early age Huntley was a predator. His first sexual adventure occurred when he was 12, when he shared kisses with his classroom sweetheart, and he rapidly progressed to much less innocent behaviour. Later he would boast how he lost his virginity at the age of 14 and, although like all of his statements this must be treated with caution, it is certainly true that he had early sexual successes. Unusually for one so young, he was attracted to girls even younger than himself. One classmate remembers: 'His technique with girls was to pick on the youngest, most easily conned ones he could find and basically just lie to them. He'd tell them anything just to get in with them, and he'd put on this really cocky manner, acting as though he was great. I could never figure out how they fell for it, but then again he did choose his victims. I can remember at least three girls he went out with at school. They were all younger than him, and none of them lasted very long.'

Huntley's exploitation of the vulnerable contained an element of savage cruelty. Although he had yet to be violent to girls, as a teenager one of his favourite pastimes was torturing animals. He would roam the streets looking for dogs and cats to feed his perverse craving. A former schoolmate said: 'The things he did were really sick. He used to strap bangers to dogs and cats to blow them up, or pour paraffin over them and set them on fire. He was always boasting about it, as if everyone would think it was great.'

25

Huntley finished his unhappy school career as soon as possible, leaving Immingham Comprehensive at the age of 16 having scraped five GCSE passes. He immediately started work gutting fish for a wholesaler in Grimsby. His working life was to show the same pattern seen in his schooldays of failing to fit in, moving from one group who refused to accept him to another, one dead-end job to the next, with bouts of unemployment in between. He would take on an incredible variety of jobs; between the ages of 16 and 20 he worked at Ross's Fish Wholesalers in Grimsby, stacked shelves at a local branch of Kwik Save, stuffed babies' nappies at the Kimberly-Clark factory in Grimsby and worked as a barman at a pub in the town.

In 1994, at the age of 20, he embarked on one of his more settled periods of employment, working at the Heinz factory in Grimsby for the next two years. He got the job there because by then both his father and mother were also working on the premises, and during this time all three would be part of the workforce. Here again Huntley was seen as a loner. Ex-colleague Stuart Rowson said: 'In factories men and women tend to have their own little groups but at break time he would sit on his own or with a very select number of friends.' All the same, Huntley seemed to be in for a more stable existence at Heinz, not least because his mother and father were with him every day.

However, this promise was not to be fulfilled, for Huntley had severe problems finding somewhere to settle. Just as he moved from job to job, so too he moved from home to home, accumulating a bewildering list of addresses. He liked to move at least every six months, and in each location he would begin anew another life of lies. He would arrive at a new flat and tell landlords and neighbours a string of falsehoods designed to enhance his reputation. Always there was the pretence of having a higher-status job or a glamorous past. He had been invalided out of the RAF, or he had worked as the manager of a large store. When the lies wore thin, Huntley moved on.

In the period 1995 to 1999 he lived in eight different locations in Grimsby and the surrounding area. Starting off at a one-bedroomed rented flat at 50 Heneage Road in 1995, he moved later that year to a room in 41a Algernon Street, a house occupied by his mother, where neighbours remember him as 'quiet'. He stayed there for less than a year, then in 1996 he was off again, this time to a very similar terraced house in Florence Street. He divided his time between there, another flat in Cleethorpes and a caravan in a girlfriend's garden. Nine months later, in 1997, he moved out and went to a rented top-floor flat in Legsby Avenue. But he again moved out within months, going to live in a flat in Veal Street in 1998. Later that year he left there and went to a new place in Abbey Drive East.

Landlord Len Smith, 65, remembered how Huntley arrived at the new flat and immediately put on yet another front. This time the future killer, always craving admiration, dressed up smartly and made out he had a professional job. Mr Smith said: 'My wife and I did not know him very well but he was very presentable and wore a suit and tie all the time. He said he worked as a rep.'

Huntley lived there from August 1998 to June 1999, before he moved away with Carr. Mr Smith and his wife Valerie, 64, remembered Huntley as taking care to make his room 'very nice'. He never brought drink into the house, and owned a large Alsatian crossbreed called Sadie. Mr Smith said: 'He had a big dog but it was always well cared for.' Mrs Smith added: 'He was a charmer. He was a good-looking lad.'

While Huntley was working at the Heinz factory and living all over town, his family began to disintegrate around him. His parents went through a troubled period in their relationship which ended in their splitting up. In 1993 Lynda, a chubby, blonde woman known for her timid character, finally decided to move away from her husband and set up home alone in Algernon Street. The separation came as a shock to Huntley. As always, he took his mother's side in the conflict, and blamed his father for what had happened. He told people his father had been carrying on with other women, an accusation which at that stage was not true. Such was the distaste Huntley developed for Kevin, he even took to using his mother's maiden name, Nixon. He regarded his Irish grandfather, Alwyn Nixon, as a far better man than his own father, who he felt had broken up the family by being too strict with his children and rejecting his wife. After Mr Nixon died, on 23 February 2002, Huntley made a pilgrimage to Ireland to attend his funeral. He always had a soft spot for the old man, a former joiner who had married twice and fathered three girls.

Following the separation from Lynda, Kevin had a series

of relationships, each of which Huntley regarded as a betrayal. The quick succession of flings culminated in the most significant affair, with Sandra Brewer, a Grimsby woman four years younger than Kevin. When Kevin met her in 1995 she was 36 and he was 40. She moved in with him almost immediately, and the couple soon left the area to live in East Anglia. They stayed together for eight years, moving between properties in Eriswell and Wangford in west Suffolk and Littleport in Cambridgeshire, seeing the rest of the Huntley family only on an occasional visit. To those who knew them they seemed a happy couple destined for a long future together, but then at Easter 2002 Kevin suddenly decided he wanted his wife back and dumped Sandra in a surprisingly brutal manner. He told her bluntly: 'I want you out and my wife back', and that was the end of their relationship.

A friend of Sandra's describes how she was immediately kicked out of the cottage in Littleport she had shared with Kevin and had to go back to Lincolnshire to find somewhere to stay. A few days later she came back to get some of her possessions. 'Kevin wouldn't even let her in the house,' the friend said. 'She had lived with him for eight years. She was shocked.' However, Sandra's shock was to turn to relief just over a year later when she discovered Kevin's son had been charged with murder. 'I'm so glad I'm not mixed up with him any more,' she told a friend. Kevin's reunion with Lynda was also to prove short-lived, for in the aftermath of their son's arrest the couple split up yet again, blaming the turmoil of events for the separation. The Sandra Brewer saga was regarded with a distaste bordering on contempt by Huntley, who saw the whole situation as an affront to his mother and therefore to himself.

Yet, while his father's extramarital adventures were to cause him problems, it is fair to say that his mother's behaviour also came as a jolt to the system. For in 1994 she met security guard Julie Beasley, who, at 21, was four months younger than her elder son. A close friendship developed which turned into a full-blown lesbian affair. This was a situation which nobody had expected; Lynda had felt no attraction towards members of her own sex before. Huntley was surprisingly accepting of his mother's new-found homosexuality. He even moved in with the lovers shortly after they began their affair, and the three became unusual housemates. They caused quite a stir among the neighbours in Algernon Street. One said: 'It wasn't the sort of thing you come across much in Grimsby. Everyone was talking about them, although they seemed nice enough to me.'

Julie, with her short, straight, brown hair and bulky figure, appeared the more masculine of the pair, with Lynda taking on the weaker role in the relationship, as she had done with Kevin. The young woman developed a good rapport with Huntley and became a popular figure with the family as a whole. The neighbour said: 'To Julie, Ian was just Lynda's son. They shared an interest in computer games and his mother's relationship didn't seem to be a problem for him.' However, Huntley still found the break-up of his parents' marriage shattering. He suffered another period of breakdown as the last pillar of his emotional security was removed. He now began to put on weight, ballooning to 14 stone and having to buy a whole wardrobe of new clothes. His medium-built, five-foot-eleven frame did not carry the extra flab well, and he looked more than a little chubby. He spent his leisure time drinking, riding a small motorcycle and playing snooker regularly. He was drifting through life.

Away from the factory floor, Huntley continued his search for vulnerable girls with a tireless trawl of the Grimsby pubs. At this time his lack of confidence led to his telling the most outrageous lies in the hope of impressing women. Too insecure to let them know he was a humble factory worker, he put on a front of arrogance and pretended to be someone else. This skill in the art of pretence was a feature of Huntley's highly manipulative character, and reflected his desire to have an impact on others by whatever devious means he could. Many who knew him felt he became so good at putting on a front that he even started to believe his own lies. Friends remember how he convincingly pretended to have been an RAF officer and slept with several girls on the strength of it. Of course, in reality the nearest he got to an aircraft was watching it through a pair of binoculars during his days spent plane spotting. Carrying out the illusion was some feat, even among the less discerning of Grimsby's young females. As one of his conquests put it: 'It sounds daft but it was easy to believe him. I think he even believed it himself, he was so into the planes and all that.'

Huntley, it seems, wanted to be someone else, and he created a fantasy world around himself in order to satisfy that craving. However transparent his lies, such was his rate of sexual success that, shortly before meeting Maxine Carr at the age of 24, he was to boast that he had slept with more than 100 women. Like everything Huntley said about himself, this was probably another lie, but there was an element of truth in it. He was enjoying what he considered to be a good hit rate, and he didn't care what extremes he resorted to in order to achieve it.

In fact, Huntley was willing to do far more than lie in order to get sex, and the sexual activities he craved were becoming increasingly abnormal. From an early age he found that the more violent and forceful his conquests the better he enjoyed the experience. Ex-girlfriends speak of a control freak who loved to dominate and abuse women. At the age of 18 Huntley seduced a 12-year-old girl and took her virginity. The child was far too young to consent; he had made a grab for her after luring her away on her own. Once he had the girl in his flat, he gave her strong alcopops until she was drunk and did not know what she was doing. He then led the staggering child upstairs to his bedroom, undressed her and took advantage of her powerless state. For her, their intercourse was painful and terrifying; for him it was an enormous sadistic thrill. Although still barely into adulthood himself, Huntley was already displaying the urges of a paedophile, desire perverted into a thirst for extreme dominance and control. Huntley liked nothing more than to force a woman to have sex with him; he was a specialist in pressurising them in a manner which bordered on rape.

Huntley met a girl called Suzanne when he was 18. She

was 16 at the time. She said: 'I met Ian through a friend and I was initially very attracted to him, but he wanted to take things further sexually and I just wasn't ready. He was a controlling, dominant personality and wanted everything his own way. He encouraged me to have sex with him.' Suzanne went out with Huntley on and off for about nine months, before dumping him for another local man in his late teens. But five years later, and while she was still seeing her new boyfriend, she would sleep with Huntley again in a drunken one-night stand. She added: 'We had been out for a few drinks and he invited me back to his place. One thing led to another and we ended up having sex. I told my boyfriend about my one-night stand and he forgave me but refused to speak to Ian again.' Huntley no doubt got a thrill out of sleeping with someone else's girlfriend; it was another example of his sexual dominance he could store away in his mind. He achieved a similar boost by burgling the flat of one of his neighbours, Lee Wood. Huntley stole jewellery and cash worth £700 from Mrs Wood's house while she and her daughter were out. He was charged with burglary after confessing the offence to police, and appeared at Grimsby Crown Court in January 1998. However, the prosecution offered no evidence and the case was allowed to lie on file. Mrs Wood believed Huntley's motive was as much malice as greed.

Huntley liked his activities to cause damage; in particular he enjoyed it when girls were frightened of him. On one occasion when he was 20 he managed to lure an 11-year-old girl into his bedroom. He had met the impressionable blonde child while on the prowl at a fun fair, and had managed to persuade her that he was her boyfriend. After enticing the besotted girl back to his flat, he kissed her and tried to pet her. When she resisted, he became enraged and locked the door, saying he would not let her out unless she let him take her virginity. He only let her go when she started to scream and he feared the noise might alert neighbours. The girl, now 20, remembers the incident with terror. Unlike Holly and Jessica, she was lucky enough to escape with her life and without being violated after Huntley, in a rare moment of compassion, relented and let her go. Another girl was 16 when Huntley managed to entice her into his flat. Again he locked her in and demanded sex, and because she refused he kept her there for two weeks. He starved her, not allowing her food or water, and after the ordeal was over she had to go to hospital. She was suffering from acute dehydration and malnutrition. The fortnight of fear had reduced her to a wreck.

Years later, following Huntley's arrest, many women came forward to tell of their horrific experiences with him. One described how she was raped by Huntley after he chatted her up during a night on the town; another told how she was also raped and reported the offence to police, only for the case to be dropped. While working at the Heinz plant Huntley became known as the factory sex pest, and at least one female colleague made complaints of harassment against him.

During his twenties, Huntley was targeting young girls with a terrifying ruthlessness, sleeping with dozens who were under the age of 16. Detectives believe he had illegal sex with up to 60 girls, the youngest being only eleven. He carried out his assaults carefully so he would not get caught. His habit was to groom his victims in a flattering, friendly manner. He would use every form of manipulation to coax them into being alone with him. In several cases he used physical force to make the girls sleep with him. Afterwards, he frightened them into keeping quiet. During this spree of sexual abuse he was reported to police eight times. He was investigated for rape four times, and on a further three occasions for having sex with an underage girl. One girl who he was accused of abusing in May 1996 was just 13. He was said to have indecently assaulted an 11-year-old girl in September 1997. Huntley was so devious that none of the claims against him stuck. When police dug up these allegations after his arrest for murder, a clear picture emerged of Huntley the serial sex attacker. But the information came too late to save Holly and Jessica.

Despite his addiction to violent sex with children, Huntley craved a stable relationship and was desperate to get married. On the face of it this seems strange but the urge for a partner was born of the same gaping flaws in Huntley's character. He needed someone he could dominate on a day-to-day basis. During his early twenties he made marriage proposals to several girls almost immediately after meeting them. At least two were turned down on the spot. Others slept with Huntley on the strength of his vows of undying love, but left him soon afterwards. Then in 1994, at the Heinz factory, he met

Claire Evans, an 18-year-old with blue eyes and curly, reddish-brown hair.

The daughter of a textile factory worker, Claire was an attractive young woman who could take her pick of men in Grimsby. She had recently been through a family crisis which left her feeling vulnerable, insecure and in need of affection. In this state she was perfect material for Huntley, who had an uncanny ability to sniff out a woman in a weakened position. The 20-year-old put on his best charm act, chatting to Claire confidently and portraying himself as a thoroughly decent young man. He asked her out and spent a large slice of his week's wage taking her on a Friday-night drinking session in the town. Friends say Claire fell for him completely; she told them she had met a man who was 'every girl's dream', fun and exciting to be with. As usual during this time of his life, Huntley proposed within days of meeting her. In a decision she would later regard as 'stupid', she accepted.

Huntley and Claire were married at Grimsby Registry Office on 28 January 1995, three days before Huntley's twenty-first birthday. The wedding was witnessed by Huntley's mother, Lynda, and the best man was his brother Wayne. By all accounts it was a low-key affair and the reception was held in a nearby pub. The couple, who had known each other for less than six months, went to live at another of the many addresses Huntley had already accumulated: a one-bedroomed flat at 50 Heneage Road, Grimsby.

Huntley began battering Claire almost from the moment he got her home. The girl, just 19 at the time, was subjected to the most horrifying ordeal of domestic violence as Huntley flew into daily rages. There seemed to be no rhyme or reason to his violence, which could erupt without warning. He would use his fists against his wife, and sometimes his feet. Her friends say he left her covered in bruises, and the only person who could protect her during the first few days was Huntley's father, Kevin. A family friend said: 'She literally had no one else to turn to, because Ian wouldn't take any notice of anyone else. He went bonkers, beating her up every day. I still can't understand why he did it, she was as good as gold to him. He must have just enjoyed hurting her, and he thought he could do that as soon as they got married. Before then he hadn't laid a finger on her, even though they had the odd row.'

Wife-battering seems to have been part of Huntley's version of a committed relationship. Although several girlfriends have said he was well capable of turning on the charm during the early stages, he almost always became violent once he thought he was in control. Later on he would commit similar acts of savagery against Carr. Unlike her, though, Claire could not put up with it, and within two weeks she had left. Huntley begged her not to go, and once more he even feigned illness, as he had done as a child, in a bid to make her stay. One night shortly before the split, he started dribbling and faked a fit. He ended up lying on the floor, his body contorted. Worried, Claire called an ambulance, but when it arrived paramedics found there was nothing wrong with Huntley.

Friends of Claire insist that it was only after leaving Huntley that she began a relationship with his younger brother. According to them, Wayne tried to help her because he was concerned at the ordeal she had suffered. He comforted her and tried to make sure she was all right, and during that process the pair fell for each other. Julie Beasley, Huntley's mother's lover, said: 'From the moment Claire and Ian met, they were always rowing. They argued more than they ever saw eye to eye. Wayne was a softy. He was sensible, had a good job as an engineer and treated Claire right, as opposed to Ian, who was a fish-factory worker and had a temper. I think in Wayne she saw what she never had in Ian, and she always got her own way. She could have anything she wanted with Wayne because he felt so much for her. It is real love between Wayne and Claire. With Ian and Claire I think it was a novelty and was never going to last. I think it hurt Ian.'

The fact that Claire left him for Wayne caused Huntley immense anguish. From the moment Wayne had come into the world Huntley had been jealous, and these feelings had grown stronger over the years; where Huntley drifted from job to job and lied to girls about being in the RAF, Wayne had forged a career with the Air Force as an engineer. Now the subject of his envy had left Huntley exposed as a failure for all to see. And that failure consisted of a rejection by a woman, something Huntley could never stand at the best of times. The humiliation hit him like a brick to the forehead.

According to Julie, Wayne and Claire kept their relationship secret from the rest of the family for a month. Then, realising he could hide it no longer, Wayne confessed to his brother at the home his mother Lynda shared with her girlfriend. Julie said: 'Wayne came round to the flat. I don't have a clue what was said. I just remember there was a lot of shouting and bellowing in the hall. Ian went mad. He went bonkers mad. He kept saying he was going to kick his brother's head in. He wanted to go after him. Wayne finally came clean and told Ian about the affair face to face because he was an honest man, and that is when the secret was out. I had been at Ian and Claire's wedding when Wayne was best man. I don't think any of us could believe what was happening. I didn't want to stick around and see them come to blows. I don't think they hit each other, but there was a lot of shouting and threats, and then Wayne left. It caused a real rift in the family. The brothers didn't speak for about a year and Ian said he wanted nothing to do with Claire ever again. I just felt sorry for Lynda because her family was never going to be the same again. She always tried to keep the peace. She hated knowing her two sons were rowing.'

Huntley was so furious over the situation that he refused to exchange a word with Claire for four years. The feud delayed the divorce as Huntley used every means he could legally to punish the couple, refusing to clear the way for them to marry. In the end Wayne and Claire had to wait until 13 January 1999 before the decree absolute was issued by East Grimsby County Court. In the meantime Huntley went round telling everyone who would listen that Claire was a 'slag' and that his brother had betrayed him. Years later, while on remand at Woodhill Prison, near Milton Keynes, Huntley would develop a paranoid belief that Wayne was poised to steal the love of his life, Maxine

Carr, as well. In a bizarre suicide note written before he tried to take his life, Huntley claimed Wayne was trying to control his fiancée. It was an odd suggestion since Carr was at that time behind bars at Holloway Prison, but Huntley was deadly serious. He also wrote in the note: 'On no account can Wayne come to my funeral.'

The fallout from a domestic situation which could hardly have been worse for a man like Huntley was to leave him profoundly disturbed. A former flatmate said: 'He was totally shattered when his wife went off with his brother. He virtually had a breakdown. He was on medication. He couldn't believe what was happening to his life. Everything he loved was upside down.' Huntley complained of several classic symptoms of depression: listlessness, an inability to get out of bed or be moved to care about anything, his own well-being included. Of course, he was a master at feigning physical and mental illness in pursuit of sympathy. His ex-wife would later tell friends that in reality his feelings were not so badly hurt. According to her, Huntley did not care so much about losing her as about losing control over her. But doctors were sufficiently worried about his state of mind to prescribe him antidepressants. He was dismayed to find the startling news of his unusual marital break-up was all over Grimsby. Another friend of the family commented: 'It was the talk of the town – everyone knew what he was going through.' Despite Huntley's obstructive behaviour, the couple did manage to marry; five years later they were joined in a ceremony at Thetford United Reform Church in Norfolk.

The elder brother must have resented the vastly different circumstances Wayne could provide. Instead of a registry office they used a country church; the groom appeared in a black morning suit with pinstriped trousers, cream waistcoat and red cravat. Claire emerged from a chauffeur-driven limousine in a white dress with long train, wispy veil, gold tiara, silver earrings and pearls. Their reception was held at the £90-a-night Bell Hotel, where the honeymoon suite contained a four-poster bed. Claire, holding her bouquet of white lilies, beamed with pride as the guests sipped champagne. Those at the ceremony managed as far as possible to ignore Huntley's pointed absence.

Huntley's method of dealing with losing Claire to his brother involved renewed attempts to seduce and dominate young girls. His delicate ego wounded, he took it out on another series of conquests, whom he treated in his normal callous manner. Friends of Claire would later point out that he made a 15-year-old girl pregnant soon after his wife left him. Two years later he seduced Katie Webber, another 15-year-old still at secondary school. Katie met Huntley, then 23, when he had left the Heinz factory and embarked on another period of moving from job to job, the work being arranged by the Maindate Employment Agency in Grimsby. Administrator Sue Penney, who used to pick Huntley up to take him to work, said he had seemed a lonely person who did a huge range of jobs before he was sacked for a 'variety of reasons', one of which was his overbearing arrogance. One of the jobs he did for a few months of 1996 was working as a door-to-door salesman selling scratch cards to raise funds for a local charity, the Handicapped Children Action Group. Katie's mother, Jacqueline, was a colleague, her role being to organise the ticket sales. As soon as he realised she had a teenage daughter, Huntley was keen to spend time with her. Before long he had made use of his connection with the family to worm his way into Katie's affections. He even moved into the four-berth caravan in the Webbers' garden.

Now a 22-year-old mother of two girls living in Cleethorpes, Katie said her first impressions of Huntley were favourable. 'Ian was nice,' she said. 'He was friendly and quite good-looking. He was a bit above himself, but he seemed interested in me. He asked me out and we started out going to pubs. He told me I was pretty and clever and that he liked me a lot. We held hands and when we sat down he rested his hand on my leg. I guess I was infatuated and young, so I was easily impressed, but I thought he was a pleasant person.' Katie felt grown-up in Huntley's presence; he took her out and treated her like an adult woman. Though she looked mature for her age, Katie was young enough mentally to find his attentions flattering. Huntley struck her as a sensitive man; he fostered this image by talking endlessly about a nervous breakdown he claimed to have suffered. He also impressed the girl by making out he used to have an important job as manager of a food store in Cleethorpes. In Huntley's fantasy world, the breakdown had forced him to give up that position.

Katie said she was totally beguiled by Huntley's act. Within just a few weeks of meeting they were having sex in Huntley's small and scruffy bedsit. Though this was a new experience for Katie, it was less exciting than she had expected. She later described the sex as 'unexceptional', 'swift' and 'ordinary'. She added: 'He seemed less interested in sex than in being in control.' Along with many of Huntley's girlfriends, she found him inadequate as a lover. Away from his preferred excitements of sadism and paedophilia, he seemed incapable of sustaining himself for more than a couple of minutes and often had trouble getting an erection in the first place.

What Huntley did get out of sex, though, was a sense of dominance. Once he had slept with Katie, his manner with her changed immediately. He became controlling and dominating, as if Katie had become his possession. She said: 'Once we'd had sex he seemed to treat me like a child; to bully me. He'd tell me who I could talk to, what I could and could not do.' Huntley tried to keep her shut away in his flat in Cleethorpes, even telling her not to go to school. He told her school would not teach her anything, and she didn't need it, because she had him. After he had kept her away from school for a week, Katie's family were visited by truancy officers and her parents appealed to Huntley to release his emotional grip on their daughter. But Huntley was having none of it. He frightened the girl into abandoning her education altogether; she left school at 15 with no qualifications and started to work packing cold cuts at a local seafood factory. 'The job was horrible,' Katie said. 'But it was what Ian wanted. He never worked, although he said I should. And he wanted me to do all the cooking and cleaning. He would lose his temper when I got it wrong. Then he started calling me stupid. I lost all my confidence as I just tried to please him.'

Katie was very close to her mother Jacqueline and her father Brian, but Huntley became insanely jealous of these bonds. He could not bear his woman to have any affection for anyone other than himself. So, if members of Katie's family called round at the flat, he would tell them she did not want to see them. If they rang, he told them she could not come to the phone. One day Katie's aunt arrived at the door. He locked his young girlfriend in the bedroom and told her aunt she never wanted to see any of her family again. After that he moved with Katie to Immingham to live once more with his mother and Julie Beasley. 'I didn't know anybody there and became totally dependent on him,' Katie said.

Huntley's father took Katie to one side and told her she should stay away from his son. His mother also told her she should leave Huntley for her own good. Always restless, Huntley soon took Katie back to Cleethorpes, where they shared a small flat. For her it felt more like a prison; he would not allow her out and he rarely had a visitor. He did not appear to have any friends, instead spending his time leafing through the pages of his many plane-spotting books or scanning the skies for different types of craft. Like many depressives, Huntley talked constantly about his past and the problems he had encountered. He hardly ever spoke of the future, never discussing what he would like to do as a job or where he would like to live.

Katie's parents insisted they were open-minded about

her relationship with her older lover. According to her father, both he and Jacqueline thought Huntley seemed all right at first, despite their misgivings about Katie being only 15. But they noticed him becoming more and more possessive. Retired factory worker Brian, 64, said: 'We tried to tell her to slow it down but Katie became besotted with him. They would row and bicker over every petty thing. He would use emotional blackmail to control her.'

In a new and sinister twist, Huntley began to beat Katie. She said: 'I remember one time when I'd put a pizza in the oven but forgotten to turn the temperature down after it had heated up. The pizza came out black and burnt. Ian went crazy and started yelling that I was stupid and useless and should be able to cook by now. Then he slapped me in the face.' Once he had started hitting her, Huntley couldn't stop. Afterwards he always said he was sorry, and pledged dozens of times to never hurt her again, but within days the promise was broken yet again and his apologies exposed as a sham. Finally, after she had been with Huntley for a year, Katie summoned up the courage to leave him. The couple had a huge row, and she lost her temper and emptied bottles of wine all over the flat. She ran outside to a phone box and called her father. She waited in the kiosk until he arrived by car to pick her up. This time Huntley did nothing to stop her from going, and she escaped from his clutches with only her pride in tatters. She did not realise how lucky she had been.

Although Huntley had claimed to be in love with Katie, he was seeing another woman within weeks. His next girlfriend was Becky Bartlett, a petite 19-year-old who had no idea what she was letting herself in for. She was shocked by how Huntley erupted into a fit of fury when she told him she might be pregnant. Becky was a next-door neighbour of Huntley's at Abbey Drive East in Grimsby when he seduced her. She said: 'He was Mr Charming when we met. I'd just split up with my boyfriend. He started taking me out and then I moved into his place. It was nice being with an older man – he was very confident. We started having sex together, but it was nothing very special. Then I realised I might be pregnant and decided to tell him. He was so angry. As it turned out, luckily I wasn't pregnant.'

Although Becky was relieved to find she was not expecting Huntley's child, another of his conquests did become pregnant and went on to give birth to a baby girl. In order to protect the child, her identity is not revealed in this book. She and her mother are among the victims of Huntley's crimes, their lives marred forever by an innocent association with his terrible acts.

While Becky and Katie felt lucky to escape from Huntley's clutches, others were not quite so fortunate. On Saturday, 16 May 1998 Huntley had been drinking his usual pints of bitter in the pubs of Grimsby, going on a crawl round his favourite haunts, including the Wine Pipe and the Mortar and Pestle. As usual, he was trawling for a girl to spend the night with, so he made sure he did not drink too much. He wanted to be in control and fully focused, ready to take advantage of any opportunity that presented itself. For Huntley, the best chance usually came in the shape of a woman who had been drinking heavily all night in the pubs that stayed open late. He would deliberately seek out those who were the worse for wear, hanging around outside the pubs around closing time and afterwards, ready to pounce on girls in a vulnerable state.

This Saturday night was no exception. Huntley was loitering in the Hollywood nightclub in Grimsby, waiting by the bar with the intent of making use of a woman under the influence of alcohol. As on many previous occasions, he managed to find a target. His eyes were drawn to an attractive blonde just 18 years old who he spotted on the dance floor. He had seen the girl out on the town the previous night, and had tried to chat her up without any success. This time he was determined to possess her by whatever methods were needed.

Although he was normally not keen on dancing, Huntley made straight for the girl, who cannot be named for legal reasons, and began gyrating clumsily next to her. She attempted to ignore him and moved away to the other side of the area, but Huntley stuck close by her and wouldn't be shaken off. Soon the slower rhythms of a love song signalled the club was about to close, and the girl made for the door. She said goodbye to a group of friends and decided to walk home alone. She had had a lot to drink, and did not notice that the man who had tried to dance with her in the club had followed her outside. The time was 2.00 am. The girl's route home was down a passageway known as Gas Alley, a cycle path which led from the Hollywood club across an area of waste ground, the site of an old railway line. It was a fine, cloudless night and the girl was in good spirits, feeling confident and unafraid despite the fact that the spot was deserted. Huntley, who had crept up silently behind her, pounced. He grabbed the girl from behind and gripped her throat with his right hand. His eyes bulging wildly, he swore at her and threatened to beat her head with a brick. He punched her in the face, yanked up her dress and tore off her tights and underwear. The girl, who was little more than five feet tall and weighed less than eight stone, tried to fight back but was overpowered by the frenzied attack. She tried to scream, but Huntley jammed his hand across her mouth as he raped her brutally. His anger satisfied, Huntley tried to persuade the girl not to report the rape, threatening to kill her if she told anyone. He began to chat more calmly, pretending nothing had happened. As he wheedled away, the girl saw her opportunity to escape and ran. Huntley decided not to pursue her, and instead walked back to his squalid flat in Veal Street. Minutes after arriving home, the girl and her distraught parents rang the police to report her ordeal.

The next day, the attack made front page news in the local newspaper, the *Grimsby Evening Telegraph*, as officers launched an appeal for witnesses. Five days later Huntley gave himself up at a local police station. He was interviewed then charged with rape. He appeared at Grimsby and Cleethorpes Magistrates' Court the following day, and was remanded in custody to Wolds Prison in Lincolnshire. A week later, at his second court appearance, he was released on bail. After another fortnight of investigation, police decided to drop the case. The decision not to prosecute Huntley left the victim, now a 23-year-old mother of one, furious and dismayed.

The publicity surrounding the case had a heavy impact on Huntley's life. Friends, colleagues and neighbours alike began to whisper that Huntley was a rapist who had got away with it. His father was later to claim that his son had suffered terribly as a result of the allegations, becoming the target of hatred and abuse from local people. Kevin said: 'It ruined his life. He lost his job, his house and everything else. He had nothing. His mother had to clothe him.' According to Kevin, the case collapsed because CCTV footage from another part of the town showed his son to have been elsewhere at the time of the rape. In reality, the case was dropped because police believed there was insufficient evidence to achieve a conviction.

What happened on the waste ground in Gas Alley was witnessed only by the rapist and his victim. And the only witnesses to any part of the night's events had seen Huntley apparently dancing with the girl in the club. Lynda Huntley claimed her son was on the verge of a nervous breakdown while on remand at Wolds, but made a sudden recovery when he was released without trial. She said, 'Someone just came up and said to him: "You are OK to go." I've never seen a man cry so much. He sobbed his heart out. He has no luck.' Although Huntley walked free amid tears of relief, the victim remained adamant that he raped her and that she was traumatised by the terror of her ordeal. Huntley had got away with it again.

4

THE MAKING OF A DESPERATE WOMAN

While Huntley was struggling through his turbulent youth, his future partner in crime was also suffering a difficult upbringing only a few miles away in the same area of the flat, industrialised landscape that is the north Lincolnshire coast. The woman who would give her boyfriend an alibi for double child murder was born Maxine Ann Capp on 16 February 1977 in Grimsby Maternity Hospital. From birth she was somewhat separated from the rest of her family, being by far the younger of two girls. Her elder sister, Hayley, had been born almost 10 years earlier, on 26 July 1967, and the age gap between them was such that they had little opportunity to share the experiences of growing up together.

Instead, Carr had the youth of an only child, and her early years were filled with feelings of separation and isolation; even at primary school she was distant from the other children and reluctant to play with them. Many who knew her as a child believed this inner loneliness was partly the product of her difficult relationship with her father, Alfred Edward Capp. Described on his daughter's birth certificate as a farm worker, he lived with her mother, Shirley Catherine Capp, née Suddaby, in a small terrace house in Yarborough Road in the village of Keelby. But, despite the arrival of their newborn child, the couple were at loggerheads, constantly rowing over the most everyday matters. By the time Carr was two-and-a-half, Alfred had split from his wife, and he would play little part in the lives of his children from then on. It seems he resented the fact that Shirley had ordered him out of the house, and he decided to cut himself off completely from her and the two girls.

From an early age she is said to have felt enormous anger towards her absent father, blaming him for all the ills in her life and in the lives of her mother and sister. It seems that the little girl felt rejected, and it would not be the first time that she found herself experiencing that emotion. She was also already showing signs of a withdrawn personality prone to severe mood swings. 'When Maxine was a little girl she was often very quiet and never said a word,' a former neighbour of Shirley's remembers. 'She looked upset a lot and sometimes she had really bad fits of temper. Most kids shout and scream a bit but she was really mad about something. I thought it was all to do with her dad, to be honest. It was difficult for Shirley being a single mum, although she did her best, that's for sure.' Following the split, Shirley took the girls to live in a council house in Keelby, three miles from the port of Immingham. Although less built up than its larger neighbour, the village is far from picturesque, made up mainly of modern brick houses with the flat, dreary lands bordering the Humber estuary stretching out in all directions. In the winter a biting east wind blows in from the North Sea across a landscape almost devoid of trees.

Shirley, who was now 33, intended to do the best she could as a single mother, even though money was scarce and the family of three had to scrape by on the wages from her job at the fish-processing plant. A stocky, chain-smoking woman with dark hair, Shirley was a popular figure among local people. By her own admission, she did not have 'two pennies to rub together'. But she remembers decorating the house to cheer up the children, filling it with her Elvis memorabilia, which included an Elvis swinging-leg pendulum clock that the girls loved. Part of the intention was to take their minds off the total disappearance of their father.

Speaking after Carr's arrest, 65-year-old Alfred said: 'I haven't had anything to do with her and that side of the family for 20 years. And I want nothing to do with them now.' Shirley was painfully aware of the gulf his absence left in her daughters' lives and felt herself partially to blame for leaving him. She tried everything to compensate, and despite having hardly any spare funds she spoilt both children as much as she could. As the baby of the family, Carr was particularly liable to play up to her mother's indulgence, and frequently made demands on her. A friend of Shirley during this period described her as: 'A kind woman who struggled to bring up her children alone.' She added: 'Maxine was quite a bit overweight and she led her mother a right dance.' Always a devoted mother, Shirley would later refuse to believe her daughter was capable of consciously providing an alibi for murder. She said: 'I can vouch for my daughter and she is innocent. She adores Huntley but she is no killer. She would not dream of hurting anyone, let alone two little girls.'

The violence and emotional power of her father's rejection set off a huge reaction in the infant Carr, for as soon as she was old enough she changed her name from Capp to Benson, and then by deed poll to Carr. 'She changed her name because Capp is her father's name and she wants nothing to do with him,' Shirley would explain. 'She changed the two ps in Capp for the two rs in Carr. She hates being called Capp – she doesn't care for her father any more. I left him when she was two and a half and single-handedly raised both her and Hayley. It was not an easy childhood but we coped.'

Between the ages of five and 11 Carr attended Keelby Primary, a small village school where all the children knew one another and felt safe. She appears to have enjoyed the company of the other children, although they remember her as a timid, quiet character. Classmate Tim Hewis recalled: 'We all had an idyllic childhood, really. The little school, this lovely village – it couldn't get any better.' Carr left the school without running into any significant problems with teachers or fellow pupils.

At the age of 11 she went to the local comprehensive,

Healing, regarded locally as a good school where teachers appreciated well-behaved pupils. Again, school proved to be an environment Carr could relate to, and she performed well in class, working diligently and achieving solid marks in tests and mock exams. Her school reports were positive and showed a good attendance record. Teachers and pupils alike remember her as a withdrawn character, polite and 'nice'. One of her best friends at school was Lisa Pogson, and Carr sometimes joined her and her family on holidays in a caravan at Primrose Valley, near Scarborough in north Yorkshire. The Pogsons remember her as polite, with no malice at all, and coming from a nice family. According to them, she was a 'genuine, honest-to-goodness girl'.

When she was 12 Carr had one of her first successes after volunteering for a community programme run by Humberside Police called Operation Life Style. She did such a good job tidying up graveyards and providing children's play equipment that she won an adventure holiday in Wales. The achievement was recorded in the local newspaper, which pictured Carr along with several other children sitting round a desk engaged in the project. In one photograph the chubby figure is seen smiling shyly as she turns to look at the camera. Another shows her proudly wearing a policewoman's hat. Unfortunately, she would not always be so eager to help the police.

Although she was doing her best to behave normally, it was around this time that Carr's inner troubles erupted into her outer world with renewed force. Entering puberty, she became acutely aware of the opposite sex. Her life so far had been spent in the company of an insular family made up of three women; her only contact with a male figure had come in the form of visits to her grandfather, Charles Suddaby, who also lived in Keelby. After her arrest he would also speak out in support of Carr, describing her as a gentle person from childhood. He said: 'Maxine always came to see me. She is a pleasant, kind girl and would not hurt a flea.'

Throughout her time at primary school and the first two years of secondary school, Carr had had little to do with boys, shunning their company. But now she began to crave the attention of a sex she had always regarded with anxiety. As she reached the age of 13 she began to feel chronically insecure about her appearance. She felt she was ugly and unattractive to boys; she thought she was too fat and spotty. The teenager became so unhappy that she went on huge eating binges to try to bring herself some form of comfort. A former school friend said: 'I remember people making fun of her because she got so fat and she ate so much. She was always eating crisps and Mars bars. She'd go into the canteen at dinner time and get two lots of chips and eat them all herself. She definitely had a problem with it.'

Carr ballooned in weight, her slight frame sometimes carrying more than 10 stone. As she guzzled more comfort food she became more and more insecure about her appearance, a feeling which in turn led her to eat again. By the time she was 15 the weight problem had reached a crisis point and she began to make herself vomit after eating. A year later this bulimia had turned into a habit of self-starvation. Carr was anorexic. Another school friend remembers the progression towards self-destruction: 'Her weight changed massively all the time when she was in her teens. She was really flabby, but then I heard she became bulimic and by 17, after she had left school, she was so skinny I didn't recognise her.' Carr had stopped trying to be a bright and helpful child, becoming even more shy and introverted, and her weight dropped to just over six stone.

Shirley was in despair at her younger daughter's condition. She tried everything to stop the cycle of insecurity which was putting the girl's life in danger, forcing her to go to the doctor, asking everybody what she could do to save the teenager. She became so desperate that she resorted to force. A neighbour remembers: 'Maxine was very ill and her mother used to have to force-feed her at times. You could hear her screaming in the bedroom.' At one point Carr was so ill that she needed hospital treatment.

Her early sex life is in many ways the opposite of Huntley's; while he made his way through dozens of girls, Carr could not manage to strike up a single relationship, even on a platonic level. The difference in sexual success is perhaps an indication of the balance of power within the relationship between the pair. More aggressive, more successful, Huntley would become, beyond dispute, the dominant partner. Carr's school friends say they cannot remember her going out with anyone. A former classmate said: 'She wasn't popular with boys – in fact, some of them used to say quite cruel things about her. They called her names behind her back because she was fat. When she got ill she was a lot thinner, but she looked even worse. People used to call her "the skeleton", which was terrible. Children can be so cruel.'

If Carr had crushes on any of the boys in her school, she didn't speak of them. She refused to indulge in gossip like the other girls, and became increasingly alienated from them as well. Instead she turned her attention to battling through her GCSE exams. For her this was something of a challenge, because she was not academically gifted. But to her credit she showed a lot of commitment, and teachers could not complain about her efforts. She gained a grade A in English Language and a B in both English Literature and Food Technology. She also achieved C grades in Geography and Science, a D in History and an E in Maths, her least favourite subject.

At the age of 16 Carr had already decided that she wanted more out of life than working in one of the many fish-processing factories in the area. She was ambitious to escape the kind of struggle that her mother had gone through over the years of her childhood, and she fixed her aim on becoming a teacher in a primary school. She was driven by a desire to better her past, but also by an interest in young children. As would be clear even at the height of the hunt for her murderous boyfriend, Carr liked to be seen as caring. She drew a sense of self-worth from the appearance of helping others. Unfortunately, Carr's need for others to value her did not extend into a genuine warmth towards them. As boyfriends would later relate, she was capable of the most extreme emotional distancing, cutting herself off from genuine feelings for someone just moments after appearing to have their interests at the centre of her world. Although disguised because of her huge insecurities, the central focus of Carr's interests was herself.

After leaving school Carr went on to study at Grimsby College, where she enrolled at the age of 17. Her GCSE grades were not quite good enough to allow her a place on the A-level courses which are part of the normal route to becoming a teacher. She opted for an NNEB childcare course, which would still put her in the right direction for working with children. She hoped it would enable her to help in the nursery class of a primary school and that she would be able to get into teaching through the back door. Sadly, these hopes suffered a setback when she was removed from the course in the first year. Teachers felt she was not up to the rigours of gaining this qualification, and was heading for a certain fail. Instead they advised her to change over to the less demanding course on general care. This she did manage to complete, leaving the college at the age of 19 with her diploma.

Armed with the qualification, Carr got herself a job at a care home for elderly people. This was close to the new home in Comber Place, Grimsby, which the Capp family had just moved into from Keelby. As a junior care assistant she earned less than £5 an hour. She became rapidly dissatisfied with the wages, and realised that the job was not helping her along the path to becoming a teacher. It was, she was forced to recognise, a dead-end job of the kind that many were used to in this working-class district. Her mother persuaded her she would be better off with a different dead-end job with higher wages. So she left the care home and went to work with Shirley at the Bluecrest fish plant in Grimsby.

Carr found the work there difficult, even though she was familiar with what went on at the factory from the experiences of her mother. She found the endless repetitive movements very boring, and daydreamed of escape. She was determined not to stay like her mother for the rest of her life in this kind of job. Another former worker who came across Carr during this period said: 'She didn't mix a lot with the others – I don't think she wanted to get involved with them because she didn't want to get stuck in the place. She wanted out from the beginning and she made no secret of it. When she did talk it was usually about how she couldn't stand the place and wanted to get away – I can't say I blamed her for that.'

A former boyfriend of Carr's also spoke of her burning ambition to become a teacher. The man, now 30, knew Carr when she was 19, when she had just begun working alongside her mother. The man, a fellow factory worker, said: 'Maxine told me about her hopes of becoming a teacher. She really was quite a mouse and a bit immature.'

As she moved into her early twenties, had managed to bring her anorexia under control. Surrounded at work by other young people, she was finally becoming confident enough to begin relationships with men. However, her adventures in this difficult territory were fraught. One of her first boyfriends was Paul Selby, a scaffolder who lived in Grimsby. She met Paul in 1997; she was 19 at the time but told him she was 23, pretending to be much more experienced than she really was. She knew Paul, who was 25, would probably have had misgivings about going out with a much younger girl. Amazingly, despite an affair lasting almost a year, Carr would never tell Paul her true age. The first he knew of it was when he read about her arrest in the newspapers and saw she was four years younger than she had made out.

During her relationship with Paul she also managed to conceal where she lived. Because she did not want him to know her flat was a dilapidated bedsit in a rundown area, she never invited him home and invented elaborate excuses to prevent him discovering her address. A few months into their relationship Carr would leave her job at the Bluecrest plant, but she didn't tell her boyfriend, and he only found out she had left months later during a chance conversation with a mutual acquaintance. Carr's behaviour still leaves Paul baffled. To this day he wonders why she concealed so much. For, despite withholding important facts about herself, Carr did not play hard to get. Very shortly after they met, the relationship became sexual.

For a while things seemed to be going well. While they were going out together the seemingly shy girl suddenly had her left breast tattooed with a stinging bumblebee. This accessory made her, for once, a centre of attention when she flashed it in a pub shortly after having it drawn. She was on a night out with Paul at the time, and he recalls feeling puzzled and disturbed by the extrovert gesture. According to Paul and others, Carr would drink large quantities as quickly as possible. Her favourite way out of her own repressed, sullen character was vodka and coke, and she would down more than a dozen in a night out in the pubs and clubs of Grimsby. When she had a few drinks inside her she would at last begin to feel comfortable in the company of men, and a totally different woman would emerge. In fact, according to Paul, she would become too comfortable with her sexuality for his liking. 'After a couple of drinks she would get up on the tables and start dancing and flashing her boobs. She was a flirt who wanted attention.'

Paul seems to have put his finger here on the reason for both Carr's flirtatious behaviour and her reticence when sober. Her preoccupation as always was with how others, particularly men, would respond to her. She craved to be attended to, to not have to suffer rejection. But both extremes were guaranteed to drive away most of the men she encountered.

After being dumped by Paul, Carr went out with his friend Daniel Hornigold, who she also managed to turn off within weeks. According to friends, she would follow Daniel around everywhere he went, whether invited or not. She would turn up unexpected while he was out playing football or in the pub. A friend of Daniel's said: 'It was pathetic. She was really desperate to be loved and kept asking if they could live together and get married. She told him she would love him forever even though they'd only been together for a few weeks. After six months he dumped her.'

Another boyfriend who had a brief relationship with Carr told how 'mouse-like' she was when sober. 'There was a group of us from the factory who would hang around together and Maxine and I dated for a couple of months. We used to go to the Wine Pipe pub in Grimsby and Maxine used to enjoy karaoke. Other than that she was quite an introvert. She was very close to her mother, who I just knew as Shirley. In those days Maxine had no contact at all with her father.' Another ex-boyfriend, Jason Wink, said he was troubled by her flirtation with other men in his presence. Factory worker Jason, 24, went out with Carr briefly just before she met Ian Huntley in 1998, and had been friends with her for a much longer period. He said: 'She loved karaoke, she was always dancing and singing. She loved being the centre of attention and would even dance on the pool table. When she was out, she was a terrible flirt. But, if you so much as looked at another girl, she would go bonkers.' The outrageous flirting accompanied by jealous reactions again seem contradictory. Yet both traits seem to have been fuelled by Carr's desperate need for the attention she had always been denied.

During this period Carr declared her new-found sexual rebelliousness by painting her fingernails and toenails black. By day she maintained her shy, nervous behaviour, but other friends speak of her different personality at night. She would go to the pub straight from work. According to Jason, their favourite pubs were the large Pestle and Mortar, in the centre of Grimsby, and the Wine Pipe in Freeman Road. Carr also enjoyed nights out at Schuberts wine bar in nearby Cleethorpes. All of these were frequented mainly by young people out to drink heavily and meet a partner for the night. Carr was mixing with a clientele dressed up in their best clothes and spending their week's wages on drinks. The thumping soundtrack towards closing time ruled out conversation. Friends say Carr was eager to join in the party atmosphere, and was often dancing on the tables.

Perhaps because of her problems in attracting long-term boyfriends, Carr revelled in male attention. One of the many who had a fling with Carr remembered: 'She was very up front about it. You didn't need to ask her twice, in fact, she asked me if I'd take her to bed. She was drunk and started dancing next to me. She wasn't my type at all, but I'd had a few as well and I just went along with it.' Her appetite for men remained a feature of Carr's personality even when she managed to secure more committed relationships. Carr did not feel guilty about being unfaithful and became expert at hiding her affairs.

Her experiment with a wilder lifestyle was reflected in another, larger tattoo of a butterfly she had drawn just below her left shoulder. She also flirted with the idea of turning herself into a biker girl and was seen riding around Grimsby on a Harley-Davidson. Yet she rarely went out without a crucifix round her neck.

Away from the bars of Grimsby, Carr didn't have many hobbies, or many friends. Problems with boyfriends erupted whenever she thought they even looked in the direction of another female. Amid these extremes of behaviour Carr's boyfriends found a lack of anything romantic; there were no cards or letters and the men felt she had no emotional involvement at all.

Even this couldn't be predicted; as Jason Wink

remembered: 'I couldn't cope with her drinking and jealous behaviour so I told her it was over quite early on. We were watching television together and I explained I felt we had no future because of her jealousy and that we should just be friends. She didn't flinch, she didn't even look at me or say a word, just kept staring at the TV. It was as if I wasn't even in the room.' Faced with yet another rejection, Carr had withdrawn into the strategy familiar in her childhood of distancing herself.

This split behaviour was puzzling to those who got to know her, partly because she would never talk about the origins of her troubles in her early life. Paul Selby felt that, whatever had happened with the extrovert girl in the pub and bed the night before, it was a very different girl who would wake up the next morning; she was an extrovert one minute and a shrinking violet the next. By day Carr seemed very inhibited and embarrassed by her body, insisting on wearing bulky woollen cardigans and full-length floral dresses. When Paul challenged her to explain her dowdy dress, she told him that she had once been raped, and this had had the effect of making her want to cover up most of the time. Later Paul came to doubt the rape had ever happened. For by night Carr changed completely. In one incident when another girl poked fun at her, saying she looked like a lesbian, Maxine just grabbed the girl's breasts. The girl was so shattered she ran off to the toilets, and Carr sat in the bar laughing uncontrollably.

Carr's intimate love life was also intense. She would deliberately try to make her lovers jealous by kissing every man she could in front of them in the course of a night out.

She would leave a bright-red lipstick brand on their cheeks, then later that night cover her lover's body in the same way. The kissing would then turn to biting, and Carr would beg her lovers to bite her back. She enjoyed the pain. Paul Selby said: 'She would beg me to bite her breasts and nipples as hard as I could. She was also into scratching me.' Carr's eccentric sexual behaviour was the source of puzzlement among her lovers. Desperate as she was to secure their affection, it seems clear that her performances were designed to please. How much she was doing what she thought they wanted, and how much of the biting, scratching and screaming was to please herself, is impossible to determine.

She prided herself on her long red fingernails, which she would use to gouge Paul's body; she wanted him to do the same. She always wore black high-heeled shoes in bed. These demands could reach the point where she was crying out for intercourse in her stilettos, on every piece of furniture in the room. Yet all this physical passion never led to any inkling of real feeling; she would just roll over, fall asleep and in the morning say: 'Bye then, are you off now?' Her behaviour left Jason Wink feeling he had been used for what she wanted at the time: sexual humiliation. 'She was always asking me to be really rough; to hurt her and perform strange sexual acts I was really uncomfortable with.'

On occasions Carr would succeed in inflicting pain; when drunk and feeling madly jealous and possessive she would fly at boyfriends with her fists and nails. She could also draw blood from other girls who had offended her. All this uncontrolled behaviour would completely disappear whenever she was introduced to the parents of her lover. Strangely, though, she would not look these people in the eye, and only answer any polite conversation with short, vague sounds.

Given her strange habits, it is perhaps unsurprising that Carr found it as difficult to hang on to her men as it had been to attract them in the first place. Without exception her boyfriends left her; she never left them. Disturbed by her behaviour, Jason Wink left her after just two months. Likewise Paul Selby was trying to get rid of her within months of their relationship beginning. But she clung on to him desperately, constantly telephoning him and tempting him back with promises of sex. Eventually Paul's only way out was to ignore her calls until she gave up. Months before that, he had left her for another woman, Patricia Hack, then 20. He even became engaged to Patricia, but still Carr would not leave him alone. She followed the couple around during their nights out, and stared at Paul suggestively. On several occasions she managed to tempt him back for illicit sex behind his fiancée's back.

These betrayals would destroy Paul's engagement. Patricia said: 'I was devastated. I was totally in love with him but all the time we were planning our wedding Maxine was sleeping with him on the side. Every time we went to the club she would be there glowering at me. She gave me the creeps. She obviously gave him something I couldn't – wild sex any time any place anywhere.' Patricia found out from neighbours that Carr made huge amounts of noise during sex with Paul. People living nearby even had to bring their children indoors to protect their ears from her howlings.

Despite the enthusiastic sex, boyfriends never felt they had reached Carr's emotions beyond anger, and didn't speak in terms of her affection or love. The man who could stir her innermost feelings of emotional attachment was still waiting in the wings for their union. Rejected by her father, she had had only a handful of lovers who had stayed with her longer than one night. Each of those had dumped her. Binge-drinking and still struggling with anorexia, she was in desperate need of somebody to support her and take her out of the drudgery of factory life, which she detested. In a precarious state, feeling severe anxiety over her future, she was to meet a man who seemed to promise a solution to her many problems. His appearance of strength and cocksure, arrogant manner would offer the promise of someone she could at last lean on. And in return for that security she would give loyalty of a kind few women would ever consider.

5

THE COUPLE
FROM HELL

With Huntley's life still in turmoil following his arrest for rape, an allegation which was eventually dropped, and with Carr feeling more isolated and rejected than ever before, both were ready and eager for a change. The chance came when the two footloose souls happened to be flung together during a pub crawl in the summer of 1998. Both were in the habit of touring the bars and clubs of Grimsby at night, and it was perhaps only a matter of time before they made contact. On this occasion, Carr was out for the night with her former boyfriend Paul Selby and a group of his friends in Hollywood nightclub, the place where Huntley had singled out his rape victim earlier the same year. Huntley, in position as usual propping up the bar and scanning the floor for female company, saw Carr and zeroed in. He knew Paul as a distant acquaintance, and used the connection to effect an introduction. Within seconds he was chatting Carr up. According to friends, the attraction was instant. Carr was bowled over by the attention of this seemingly charming man and was drawn to his self-certain, arrogant manner. Before the night was over he had asked her out, and days later they were having sex.

Carr was on the rebound from the recent breakdown of her short relationship with Jason Wink, and was eager to make this new affair more lasting. Huntley began inviting her out after work every night, and was soon meeting her regularly in Grimsby, on the circuit of pubs they both knew. He spent more and more time with Carr, becoming an important figure in her daily life. Carr, who was still living with her mother, Shirley, in a £45-a-week three-bedroom council flat at Comber Place, was working as a fish gutter at the Findus plant. Huntley had just ditched his similar job at a fish processing factory in Caistor, 10 miles inland from Grimsby, and had clinched a temporary post as a supervisor in an insurance company in Market Rasen, Lincolnshire. His escape into a better job was the stuff of dreams for Carr, and she was easily impressed by his boasts about the importance of his new position.

Seeing them together in the Grimsby nightspots, many who knew Huntley thought he was just carving yet another notch on his bedpost. But as the pair spent time together they found they had a great deal in common. They came from similar backgrounds and they had been brought up a few miles apart, having even briefly attended the same school, and had worked at the same Bluecrest plant in the town. More importantly, both had suffered the pain of failed relationships and were troubled by profound insecurities stretching back into childhood. They recognised something in each other which drew them close. For better or for worse, they had met their match. Not only was Carr attracted by the same charm that had secured Huntley his many conquests but she was also attracted by the possessiveness that Katie Webber had ultimately fled from, seeing it as a sign of devotion. In the embryonic stages of her first serious relationship, Carr was quickly intoxicated by Huntley's attention. Over drinks they talked about their past problems with a freedom neither had experienced before, and within only a few days the connection grew so strong that they decided to live together. Carr jumped at the chance to move in with a man who seemed to provide her with the security she had craved for so long. She moved into Huntley's £50-a-week flat in Veal Street, near the centre of Grimsby. Only a few months before, while living at the same address, he had been charged with rape, and spent time in jail on remand, before being released without charge through lack of evidence. But despite, the fact that the whole town knew of at least some of the events in Huntley's history, Carr chose to ignore them. She never questioned Huntley, but rather clung to him with a rapidly growing devotion.

Caught in a fantasy world alongside Huntley, before long she was gazing into his eyes with the kind of loving dedication Huntley had never before succeeded in fostering. Carr's mother would later speak of this blind loyalty. Following her daughter's arrest, Shirley said:

'Maxine is in love with the man. Nothing will break them. She adores the ground Ian walks on. Maxine thinks the world of him – she would do anything for him. Maxine is standing by Ian – she is standing by him for reasons even I do not know. They did break up for a while recently and she was heartbroken. Then they seemed happy again. He often drives her up to see me and drives her back down to Cambridgeshire.'

The couple's exclusive devotion to each other only encouraged them to retreat further from the society around them. Huntley spent less and less time outside his shabby bedsit, going out only for work and the very occasional few pints in the pubs of Grimsby. Never one to make friends, he cut himself off even from the acquaintances who had seen him regularly on Friday and Saturday nights. Likewise Carr removed herself from the circles she had been out with on a regular basis. According to friends of Carr's mother, Huntley did not like Carr going out on her own. If she was not at home when he got back from work, he would work himself up into a jealous rage. Shirley complained that she saw less of her daughter after Carr began living with Huntley. Mother and daughter had always been close to the point where friends described them as 'inseparable', but Huntley seemed to feel this family tie was a threat to his own status as the most important person in his girlfriend's life. Just as he had done with Katie Webber, he tried to separate Carr from her family.

With Carr secured to him by a potent mixture of emotional dependence and domination, Huntley no longer needed to impress other women with his lies. But he remained driven by a desire to project an image of himself which would make others envious. His ridiculously overblown stories continued: he claimed to have been thrown out of the RAF because of his asthma, that his father had died when he was a child, that he was training to be a professional bodybuilder and even that he and Carr had won the Lottery. As if he were running some kind of public-relations operation to boost his reputation, Huntley also made maximum use of his new domestic situation. He liked to flaunt the fact that at last he had a long-term, live-in girlfriend who actually seemed to want to stay with him. After the much-publicised disaster of his earlier marriage and the failure of all his other relationships with women, he boasted as much as he could about this latest partnership. He spoke of Carr as 'the missus' and would talk about his domestic arrangements at length to anyone who had the patience to listen. A former colleague at the Bluecrest plant remarked on the sudden change in his behaviour: 'Huntley was always going round acting like he was Jack the Lad, then after he met her he started to pull this "I'm a married man" thing. He went on and on about Maxine cooking for him and cleaning his place and doing this and that for him in bed. He talked about her as if she was like a cross between a sex slave and a cleaning woman – he loved it.'

As usual with Huntley, the compulsively fabricated public image concealed a private reality far less perfect. Behind the closed doors of their Veal Street bedsit, he and Carr were having screaming matches on a daily basis. Neighbours said their ferocious rows were often accompanied by the sound of plates and glasses being smashed. As he had with Katie Webber and others before, Huntley quickly became violent, while Carr, a shrinking violet in the street, was capable of astonishingly loud raging and howling behind closed doors. One neighbour who lived in Veal Street at the time said: 'We used to hear terrible rows and screams coming from their house. She would be crying, he would be screaming, and it used to go on through the night. They were the couple from hell and you would not want to live next door to them. But, if you passed them in the street, you would not think they would be capable of such violent outbursts. He seemed a little bit timid and she was very quiet.'

In March 1999 Huntley started work at ICF Loans, a finance company based in Binbrook, Lincolnshire. Former colleagues there remember how he would parade his cruelty to Carr and show off the power he had over her. 'He liked to boast about humiliating her,' one said. 'He'd call her up in front of everybody and shout out, "Have you cleaned my f***ing house yet, you useless lazy bitch?" or "Have you made my tea yet, you stupid cow?" He'd call her a slapper and a slag and then put her on speakerphone so we could hear her saying she was really sorry and she knew she was lucky to have him. She would be in tears on the end of the line, then he'd put the phone down and burst out laughing. I've never seen anything like it – everyone was shocked.'

Shirley Capp's neighbours in Comber Place said Carr would frequently flee to safety, returning home to her mother after her violent rows with Huntley. According to them, she would often wear sunglasses in an attempt to hide black eyes, and she would also be seen with swelling around her nose and cheeks. A friend of Shirley's said: 'Everyone knew that he beat her up. That was his way of finishing off a row, hitting her just like she was a man. He was a really nasty piece of work. Shirley was very upset every time Maxine came home like that – she didn't know what to do about it.'

Following every row, Huntley would use his charm to talk Carr round. 'When she is up here, he is always on the telephone to her,' said Shirley. Much of that time on the telephone was taken up with Huntley's apologies. As with his other girlfriends before, he would always tell Carr he was so sorry, he didn't know what had come over him and he wouldn't do it again. The patter was the classic behaviour of the wife-beater. Another of Shirley's friends, Maria Pawson, 45, remembered the impact of Huntley's violent behaviour: 'Maxine's mother would come to see me in floods of tears. She would say to her daughter, "Leave him, he's no good", but Maxine wouldn't listen. He had a hold on her and she was utterly besotted with him. Soon after meeting Ian, Maxine left her mother's flat and they moved in together. But every two weeks Maxine was back at her mother's because they had had a row. They were always arguing but he always managed to get her to go back by telling her he loved her – she believed it. In the end Shirley refused to let Ian into her flat.'

Those who knew the couple commented that he treated her 'like a lapdog'. He thought nothing of cheating on her with other women. From the beginning of their relationship he was two-timing her with an underage girl. She was still at school and studying for her GCSEs when she met Huntley in a nightclub soon after her fifteenth birthday. She said: 'He was nice to me at first. Then I discovered he was two-timing me with Maxine.' Carr also discovered the deception, and sank into a depression. But she didn't leave. Her willingness to inflict harm on herself was graphically illustrated on two occasions when Huntley tried to leave her. Beside herself with grief, and wanting to prove she would make the ultimate sacrifice to bring her man back, she attempted suicide. After one attempt doctors rushed to save her life and she spent several days in hospital.

Despite the breakdown of their relationship, Huntley rushed to her side. Suicide attempts were nothing new to Huntley; he knew what it felt like to want to take one's own life. Where Carr's intense behaviour would have driven many other men away, it attracted Huntley like a magnet. Convinced Carr was willing to die for him, he came back to her. And, where others would have been ashamed of driving a woman to such drastic measures, Huntley saw Carr's suicide attempts as something to brag about in front of everyone at work.

Had he known the full facts about Carr's behaviour during their relationship, Huntley may have been less inclined to boast. For the same insecurity which drove her to attempt suicide also inspired her to cheat on him, and Carr continued to sleep with new and past lovers. During periods when Huntley was unfaithful to her, Carr responded by returning to the Grimsby club scene. Even when her relationship with Huntley appeared to be working, she still found it difficult to refuse approaches from others. But on an emotional level she was lost without the man she called her 'partner'.

One of Carr's desperate cries for help and attention was provoked by Huntley's relationship with a 24-year-old, a girl a year younger than her and by several accounts much more attractive. Huntley became so enamoured of the girl he had met during a return to his haunts in the nightspots of Grimsby that he left the flat he shared with Carr and moved in with her. They lived together in a flat in the Lincolnshire village of Brigg. But, though he was able to leave Carr physically, he remained emotionally tied to her. Huntley's new girlfriend claimed he was 'obsessed' with Carr and talked about her constantly, going over her problems and the problems the couple had together as though this new girlfriend was nothing more than a shoulder to cry on.

Characteristically, Huntley began to subject her to an array of controlling demands. A close friend of hers said: 'At one stage he told her not to answer the phone. He said it was because his mum might be ringing, but she always suspected it was Maxine he was waiting for. She was always on his mind. She suspects he continued the relationship with her behind her back. Their bond was too intense for her. She didn't want to know any more.' As Huntley rushed off to Carr's bedside after her suicide attempt, his new girlfriend decided enough was enough and expelled him from her life, ending the relationship in November 2000.

Try as he might, Huntley found he could not leave Carr. For this man whose former wife had left him for his brother, a woman who seemed willing to die for him, staying with him whatever he did, through violence and outright rejection, was what his fragile ego craved. The pair decided to make a new go of their relationship.

Grimsby, the town of all Huntley's failures, remained an overwhelmingly depressing place. Hoping to put an end to their past problems, in June 1999 the pair moved to a ground-floor flat in West Street, Scunthorpe. The effects of yet another new beginning at first seemed constructive. Their landlord, Paul Dickson, 28, said: 'When they moved in I thought they were really nice and they seemed so happy together.' In this atmosphere of relative harmony, Huntley felt he needed to offer his girlfriend more commitment and to put his infidelities behind him. Anxious to end his string of failures and to keep hold of Carr, he borrowed £4,000 to buy her an engagement ring and proposed. According to Andrew Brookes, a neighbour in Scunthorpe: 'Ian was having a bad time with Maxine and was desperate to put a smile on her face. He got a loan and picked out a diamond and gold engagement ring. Maxine was delighted. It was smashing.'

Huntley had resorted disastrously to marriage proposals at least three times before, but this time it seemed different. It seemed like love. Not the fleeting passion he had felt with Claire Evans, but something much deeper, more mature and enduring. Here was a woman who would not leave him for the world, who made his life more stable than ever before. And, as Huntley got down on one knee, the hollowness inside Carr which had grown as a result of rejection after rejection melted away. This man, she decided, was the love of her life and she would accept his offer of marriage. Two years later, as the couple stood side by side in the dock, perhaps she saw things differently.

Carr proudly showed off the gaudy diamond ring to her mother. With the same loan money Huntley also chose his and hers designer watches for them both, and spent the rest on a red, J-registration Ford Fiesta. For a brief time at least, things seemed to be getting better. Cheered by the engagement, Carr's mood lightened, and neighbours remarked that she seemed content and optimistic. She'd spent years of her life doubting whether she was worth anything, but here at last was the proof that she was. Standing by Huntley had paid off; her extreme loyalty had brought her the support she needed. As for Huntley, the ring meant ownership. Carr was his and now everyone would know it.

However, keeping Carr meant so much to him that he had borrowed beyond his means. Debt collectors threatened to burst the bubble of the couple's brittle happiness. Andrew Brookes said: 'He was having problems paying the loan and they left suddenly without telling me. I think he must have had a real nightmare with the loan.' Landlord Paul Dickson also had reason to believe Huntley was experiencing financial difficulties. 'I thought he was trying to dodge something. We've had letters for him from banks and debt-collection companies.' Huntley tried to ignore the warnings, but they kept coming. Unable to pay back the loan, he opted for his usual strategy of running away. In 2000 the pair suddenly moved 15 miles to a flat in the High Street of the village of Scotter, near Gainsborough, Lincolnshire. The new start in Scunthorpe had been a false dawn, and the pattern of restlessness continued. Huntley's proposal and extravagant borrowing had failed to straighten out their lives.

The couple's neighbours in Scotter reported a familiar story of rows and social detachment. Huntley found work as a security guard and Carr as a hotel receptionist, but neither vocation provided the fulfilment they craved, and within months the debt collectors had tracked them down to their new address. The idea of reinventing themselves continued to prove attractive. In a characteristic piece of fantasy, they told neighbours they would be moving to America, because Huntley had secured a job there. The truth was they had begun to look into the possibility of starting afresh, in a new part of the country where the future was open.

In 2001 the couple moved south to East Anglia. As they searched for permanent employment, Huntley worked in a local pub. Soon came the break they had been waiting for – through his father, a caretaker at a primary school in Littleport, near Ely, Huntley learnt in the summer of a vacancy 10 miles away, at Soham Village College, for the same post as his father's. Seizing the opportunity, Huntley and Carr arrived in Soham to find a small, attractive town in the centre of productive, low-lying farmland, famous for root crops and fruit.

In the south-east corner of Cambridgeshire, near the Isle of Ely and the border with Suffolk, Soham is a large parish of reclaimed fens and meres. A far cry from grimy Grimsby, the town has charm and beauty, with its far horizons and clear night sky, devoid of the orange glow of urban life. Despite its long and rich history, dating back at least as far as AD 630, when St Felix is said to have founded a monastery there, Soham has not become a tourist trap. It has retained a sense of character the outside world has not corrupted. At the same time it is not an isolated spot – Cambridge is a short drive to the south-west, and London only 70 miles away.

Huntley started work at Soham Village College in September 2001, at the beginning of the school year. The college was a mixed comprehensive grant-maintained school of around 1,300 pupils, which had gained a reputation for high academic results, and for excelling in sports and the arts. The couple moved into the tied caretaker's house on the premises, at 5 College Close. The college was eager to make as certain as possible that the new caretaker would not be the cause of any problems. Huntley's new employers were reassured by the fact that he was in a settled relationship. They were also aware that he had no previous experience as a caretaker. Because of Huntley's lack of experience, the college insisted on his serving a probationary period as a volunteer. So he started work there in an unpaid capacity and remained in that position for three months while the authorities made up their mind whether he was the right man for the job.

When he arrived, Huntley began work under the name Ian Nixon, which he had been using for much of the time since his parents split up. Along with everyone else who works in schools across the country, he was put through the police checking system. The police found no criminal record under the name Ian Nixon, or Ian Huntley or any history which would suggest Huntley was unsuitable for work with children.

Although Huntley had been investigated over several sex attacks in Grimsby, he had never been convicted. Because the cases against him had failed, he did not have a criminal record and so was not identified as a risk during the vetting process. Later, a public inquiry was mounted into how Huntley had managed to slip through the checks and get a job working with children.

Having satisfied the college with his performance on site and in the interview, Huntley was given the title Residential Senior Site Officer in December 2001. He was head of a team of four employees who cared for the college and its grounds. His salary was £16,000 a year and he was allowed to rent the three-bedroom detached home at the subsidised rate of £25 a week. A month short of 28, Huntley felt that at last he had in some way succeeded.

After moving restlessly from job to job, from home to home and from relationship to relationship, Huntley finally had the opportunity to settle down. He had also forged something of a reconciliation with his father. The fact that Kevin had spotted the caretaker vacancy for him made Huntley feel warmer towards a figure he had barely spoken to for large stretches of his life. This process of becoming closer to his father was made easier by a dramatic turn of events at Easter 2002. Kevin suddenly decided he had had enough of his lover, Sandra Brewer; he threw her out of his tied caretaker's cottage in Littleport and invited his wife, Lynda, back to live with him. She accepted Kevin's approaches, and by the beginning of May Huntley's parents were man and wife once more. Huntley had always blamed his father for separating from Lynda. He was delighted that at last the rift had been healed; the anger he had harboured towards his father for years began to dissolve.

Huntley celebrated the recreation of his family with the symbolic gesture of dropping the surname Nixon and accepting his father's once more. He also began to see more of his brother, Wayne, and took a few tentative steps towards forgiving him for taking up with his ex-wife, Claire. Wayne lived only a few miles away in the Suffolk town of Brandon, and worked as an engineer at RAF Mildenhall. Far away from the Huntley family's origins in Grimsby, it seemed for the first time that the clan might one day bury its divisions. Perhaps they could live happily together in this new, less hostile location.

While Huntley's dreams of matrimonial happiness and a united extended family seemed within his grasp, Carr also found reason to hope that in Soham some of her dreams would come true. When the couple first arrived there she had yet to find a job in the area. After four months of searching, in February 2002 she managed to get a temporary post as a teaching assistant in classes 11 and 12 at St Andrew's Church of England Primary School. All her life Carr had wanted to be a teacher, and now this ambition appeared to be in sight. For her the part-time job would be a means of getting into the profession by the back door. Then she could put her academic failures behind her, because they would no longer matter. In truth, life for Carr had never been better. Soon, she hoped, she would have her dream job, a home, a husband and perhaps children of her own. On taking up the teaching post, she was, like Huntley, subjected to a police check. This was likewise restricted to her current name. Her original surname, Capp, was not searched and, even if it had been, the police would not have found any record of criminal or dangerous behaviour.

Huntley's new employers were pleased with his efforts, describing him as a good worker. Geoff Fisher, 54, Holly and Jessica's head teacher, said Huntley seemed to be making a good start at the school: 'He was picking up a big job for us and was learning the ropes but seemed to be doing well. There was not a glimmer of reservation with him on a personal basis by either staff or pupils.' Huntley was indeed popular with many pupils, particularly the girls. The fact that he, younger than most of the teachers, had good relations with the pupils led his employers to put him in charge of supervising children during detention. The mother of one girl who was supervised by Huntley said the pupils thought he was 'cool, quite hip-hop'. She said that he would joke and tease the girls over their punishment. Wendy Dobson, 32, who lived a few doors down College Close from the couple, said Huntley supervised her 14-year-old daughter when she had detention on her own. As always he strove to be impeccably polite and amiable in public, to present a picture of normality and respectability. His charming manner led many naïve young pupils to warm to him.

However, his charm was not quite so effective with some of the teenage boys at Soham Village College, who grew uneasy about him, seeing cracks in his façade. On occasion his volatile temperament showed through, as he would shout alarmingly at them for even the slightest contravention of school rules. At the same time his friendliness with the girls developed an edge of flirtatiousness which angered the boys. Speaking days after Huntley's arrest, one male pupil said: 'We never liked him since he started. We never knew she, the fiancée, existed until Friday. From the moment he came to the school, we thought he was strange. He used to go around being strict about uniform with the boys, telling them to do up top buttons, but he would never do the same with the girls.'

While some pupils had misgivings about Huntley, Carr was experiencing unprecedented popularity among the pupils of St Andrew's Primary School. She was able to revert to her childhood, a time before anorexia and problems with boyfriends had begun to plague her. With children she felt comfortable; with adults she felt challenged. She grew close to the pupils in a way most adults would struggle to achieve, tuning into their way of thinking. For Carr it was therapeutic, almost a healing process. One member of staff at the school remembered how she seemed far more at ease with the children than with the other teachers. 'She really got on well with the kids – it was like she couldn't take enough trouble to make them happy,' she said. 'But with the staff she was quite shy and nervous and didn't make any friends. She didn't seem comfortable with anybody over the age of 11.'

Both Huntley and Carr failed to make close friends in their new surroundings. But, with a new level of stability and success, the couple opened up to a degree that they had never been able to achieve back in Grimsby. As the months went by they blended in with the townspeople to the point where they were on chatting terms with most of the neighbours, parents of children at the school and shopkeepers. Huntley and Carr had never experienced the warmth that the local people showed towards them. One described Huntley as a 'trendy, friendly man who was good with kids and used to walk his big black Alsatian in the grounds.'

Huntley would visit the nearby bakers, Fullers, every day to get a working lunch while Carr was teaching. His order was always the same: a slice of pizza, a doughnut and a can of Pepsi. 'He was always pleasant and we never doubted him,' an assistant said. 'When he smiled butter wouldn't melt.' On Saturdays he would go to the Handy Plaice chip shop off Soham High Street, habitually wearing an England football shirt and tracksuit trousers. As summer came and the couple became part of Soham life Carr hoped to be taken on permanently by the school the following academic year. She applied for a permanent job, but was turned down following an interview. Mr Pearson said, on behalf of Cambridgeshire County Council: 'She did not get the job because there was a better candidate.' It was clear evidence that, while popular with the children, Carr did not get on so well with the staff.

Nevertheless, by the summer of 2002 Huntley and Carr had achieved an appearance of normality and stability which endeared them to the friendly people of Soham. From the outside at least, there were few hints of the past they had tried so hard to escape from. Despite Carr's failure to secure the job she so desperately wanted, the couple had never been happier. Proudly wearing her engagement ring, she was optimistic about the future.

What nobody could see was that a stable relationship was not enough for Huntley. He was on the brink of committing horrific acts. Routine was the only thing which kept him on a level; and, as school broke up for the long summer holiday, his disturbed mind began to race. The time bomb was ticking.

6

THE FAMILIES

While Huntley and Carr got on with their dysfunctional relationship, their victims remained completely unaware of the danger on their doorstep. The Wellses and the Chapmans had no reason to believe Huntley was anything other than a friendly, familiar figure; to their unsuspecting eyes, there was nothing more unusual about him than a Lincolnshire accent. For while Huntley's mind was haunted by paranoia, depression and violent mood swings, both the Wellses and the Chapmans inhabited a territory far less sombre. Where he and Carr were so itinerant that they hardly spent more than six months in the same place, the two families were the epitome of solidity, remaining in Soham for most of their lives. And where Huntley and Carr came from turbulent family backgrounds, the Wellses and the Chapmans were both stable, established couples with the support of large extended families behind them. In these and in many other ways the contrast between the criminals and their victims could hardly have been more stark.

Kevin and Nicola Wells and Leslie and Sharon Chapman had had fortunate, happy and stable existences prior to the bombshell that hit them in the summer of 2002. Thirty-eight-year-old Kevin and Nicola, three years younger, grew up together in the Soham area; friends described them as 'thoroughly happy' and 'inseparable'. Soon after their marriage they were blessed by the arrival of their son, Oliver, and then two years later by the birth of Holly. It was a balanced family of four which everyone found charming to meet.

Holly, 10, and Oliver, 12, had benefited throughout their early childhood from the presence of a large extended family. Kevin's father, Gerald, 69, known as Tinker, and his mother, Agnes, 61, or Aggie as she was known around Soham, would often babysit the children and visited the couple regularly. Kevin's brother, Andy, and Nicola's mother, Diane Westley, 60, were also part of the Wells children's daily lives. The strength of these family bonds was to be vividly illustrated in the weeks following the tragedy; even in the midst of despair the Wellses were able to pull together. Diane spent so much of her time at her daughter's home that August that she seemed to have moved in. Gerald and Agnes likewise became pillars of strength for the Wellses, present at many a grieving gathering or listening to tearful phone calls.

As well as their close family, Kevin and Nicola also had

plenty of friends. They were among the most popular inhabitants of the town, often at the heart of local events. On the night when Holly and Jessica disappeared they had been holding a barbecue for their friends Rob and Trudy Wright, and this sociable way of spending a Sunday was typical of the couple. Always outgoing, they played host many times a year. Kevin and Nicola had the habit of going to worship at St Andrew's Church on Sundays, and were popular among the congregation.

In his younger days Kevin had been a key player for Soham Town Rangers Football Club, and even as he approached 40 he still played the occasional game. He was the captain of Ely and Haddenham Cricket Club, a successful town team which plays to a high standard. As captain, it was his responsibility to get involved in all the social events organised by the club, a task he relished.

Kevin, a bald man of medium height and slim build, appeared at times a serious character, especially to those who didn't know him well. But, once involved in the spirit of a party, he was a cheerful, optimistic type, full of humour. His manner of speech also seemed at first quiet and sensible, but it was confident too, expressing an inner belief in his abilities. His interest in cricket and football was reflected in his dress, which often consisted of soccer strips, sweatshirts, tracksuits and trainers. In the homes, shops and pubs of Soham, Kevin was an extremely well-known and well-liked figure. It was hard to find anyone in the town who did not class themselves as a friend of his at some level.

The enterprise Kevin showed on the sports field was

reflected also in his working life. He set up his own contract window-cleaning business, K Wells Cleaning Services, a small but highly successful operation. Kevin's many friends said he was devoted to his wife, a slim, even-featured woman with short brown hair. Nicola was quieter and less outgoing than her husband, but equally courageous and determined in her own way. With her working as a legal secretary, the couple managed to save up enough money to buy one of the better properties in Soham, a four-bedroomed detached modern house with a large back garden and front lawn in a quiet cul-de-sac, Red House Gardens. The house, in dark-red brick, was worth around £170,000, and had every modern convenience, from double glazing to central heating. As with everything in their lives, the Wellses kept their house immaculately and the lawn at the front, punctuated by carefully weeded flower beds, was clipped tidily around the edge of the neatly laid patio. Despite their financial success, the Wellses did not consider themselves aloof from the rest of Soham in any way. They were known as very down-to-earth people.

About five minutes' walk away from the Wellses' home, the Chapmans lived in a semi-detached four-bedroomed property in Brook Street. The row of houses of which this was one stretched the length of a long road that ran parallel to the main route through Soham but on the outer edge of the town. These houses were older than the Wellses', dating back to the 1930s. The Chapmans' home was pebble-dashed and painted white at the front, and had been modernised with double glazing and aluminium window frames. A little less affluent than the Wellses, they were also an older family, with Leslie being 51 and Sharon 43.

A stockily built man with greying dark hair and a moustache, Leslie was an engineer by trade and was due to start a new job in a local factory the day after his daughter was kidnapped. Sharon, of medium height and build with short, dark hair, was a learning support assistant at St Andrew's Primary, where Jessica was a pupil. Her job meant she was a colleague of Carr's from the time she started work there in April. The two women worked in similar part-time roles, supporting the main teaching staff, and in the small school they came across each other every day.

As Sharon put it: 'I would see her on a daily basis and talk to her about school issues and sometimes we would discuss Jessica. Jessica thought Maxine Carr was the best teacher she had ever had. She thought she was cool. Carr used to help Jessica with homework and coursework, and Jessica did genuinely think a lot of her.' Sharon's contact with her colleague was another of the links between Huntley and Carr and their victims which was inevitable in a town the size of Soham. Not that the Wellses and the Chapmans rubbed shoulders socially with the caretaker and his girlfriend; for them he was something of an outsider. But both sets of parents were well aware of the new man looking after the grounds of their daughters' school, and had seen him performing his duties there on many occasions.

The Wellses and the Chapmans were warm people, welcoming everyone, and they passed the time of day with both Huntley and Carr on several occasions, from their arrival in the town in September 2001 until the murders of their daughters 11 months later. Kevin in particular had many encounters with Huntley, because his cleaning business had a contract to work at Soham Village College. He first met the caretaker just before Christmas 2001, and knew him as 'Ian'. Like the Wellses, the Chapmans were long-established residents of Soham, and had been living in their Brook Street home for a decade. Leslie, who speaks with a slight Cambridgeshire accent, had lived in the area all his life. Sharon too was a local woman, whose parents, Richard and Barbara Elsey, lived in the nearby village of Isleham, although Barbara originally came from Manchester. Although well liked in the town, the Chapmans were less outgoing than the Wellses, and tended to keep themselves to themselves to a greater degree. This difference between the two families was reflected after the bodies of the girls were discovered. While the Wellses' home was full of friends and family members who had come to share their grief, the Chapmans withdrew to mourn in their own private space, bolting the door and drawing curtains over the windows.

Jessica grew up as the youngest of three girls, very much the baby of the family. In August 2002 her sister Rebecca was 16 and her other sister, Alison, was 14. Both were very close to Jessica and following their examples made her mature and sensible for her age. This well-behaved nature was what made her disappearance on Sunday, 4 August so much out of character. While away from home, Jessica would use her mobile phone eight or nine times a day to ring her mother. She was allowed to visit only a few friends' homes by herself, a short list of locations which included Holly's house. On the Sunday she disappeared, Jessica had rung Sharon twice during the day, letting her know she was at Holly's, giving her friend a present bought on holiday in Minorca. This sensible behaviour was the product as much of Jessica's nature as of the drilling about stranger danger her parents had given her.

She was a very lively child, a healthy, outdoor girl who enjoyed playing the tomboy. She liked sport of all kinds, and played football for Soham Town Rangers girls' under-11s team. She also loved swimming and went for regular training sessions with the Cambridgeshire Swimming Group, representing her county on several occasions. Of average height for her age, being four feet six at the time of her disappearance, she had an athletic build. In keeping with her sporty personality, she shunned girly clothes like frilly dresses and was more often seen in tracksuits and T-shirts, her hair tied back in a ponytail or under a baseball cap. A pretty little girl with shoulder-length, light-brown hair, an upturned nose and shining brown eyes, she was bright and did well at school. She liked music as well as sport and was a fan of S Club Seven and Steps. She was still afraid of the dark, and slept with the light on. She was also afraid of dogs, and would run away and scream if she came across bugs and spiders. Her sister Rebecca said: 'We have a typical big sister relationship. I always do her hair and she asks my advice on what to wear. She is loud, chatty and has a very bubbly personality. She is very popular at school and has lots of friends.' Growing up in Soham, Jessica did not have the hard-headed mentality of an inner-city child. But she had learnt a lot from her elder sisters, and was far from naïve. As Leslie put it, 'She's not streetwise but she's not stupid either.'

Jessica met Holly when the pair were both four years old and attending nursery school. They struck up an instant and close friendship. Another of Holly's friends, Natalie Parr, 10, described how the two were 'like sisters'. Speaking after their disappearance, she added: 'They are always playing together and they are best friends.' The girls had very different characters; where Jessica was something of a tomboy, her friend was extremely feminine, wearing skirts rather than tracksuits and enjoying dressing up, dancing and playing with make-up.

In the days following the girls' disappearance, Holly's parents released photographs of her to try to jog people's memories in the hope that someone somewhere had seen their daughter. One of these shows Holly dressed as an attendant to the Carnival Queen at the 2001 Soham carnival. Holly, who was a majorette, was in her element dressing up in costume and having her hair plaited for the event. Another picture shows her in a flowery swimsuit while on holiday; again the girly design was typical of her taste.

Although Holly also liked sport, it was less important to her than it was to Jessica. She liked to watch Kevin playing football, and the red David Beckham shirt she was wearing on the night she vanished was one of her favourite pieces of clothing. Both girls idolised the England captain as their hero and were committed Manchester United supporters because of his membership of the side. Like Jessica, Holly was a strong swimmer. A blonde, fair-skinned girl, she was of average height for her age, at four feet six inches, but was slighter than Jessica. She also had a small white birthmark on the right of her forehead, just below the hairline.

Kevin, who would later write a poem in his daughter's memory characterising her as the 'Soham rose', described Holly at the time of her disappearance as a 'fantastic girl'. 'She is bright, bubbly, vivacious, very intelligent,' he said, and almost everyone who met her seems to have agreed. Known in Soham for her ever-smiling appearance, she had many friends among the other children, although none who challenged Jessica as her favourite. As her mother pointed out, she was a pretty child. 'She has straight blonde hair which is more blonde in the summer than in the winter,' Nicola said. 'She is very pretty and her eyes are blue-green-grey, very difficult to describe.'

Like Jessica, Holly was a sensible, mature girl. Her aunt, Lesley Allen, said: 'She is the most sensible well-behaved 10-year-old you could imagine. If Holly was going to be a minute late she would phone home.' Holly's parents had made her aware of the dangers of talking to strangers or being away from home. They would not allow her to go out without her telling them exactly where she was going, and much of Soham was out of bounds. They allowed her only to visit the homes of children whose parents they knew well, and on occasion she was permitted to go into the centre of Soham to buy sweets with her £3-a-week pocket money, but only if she asked first. Her headmaster, Geoff Fisher, said she and Jessica had both been taught at school never to approach strangers. 'The possible danger from strangers is something we have impressed upon them from a very early age.'

Although taught to be wary of some adults, Holly and Jessica were both known as very well mannered. Heather Brasher, 56, who owned a craft and gift shop in Soham, recalled: 'Holly and Jessica often came into the shop and browsed. They were wonderfully polite and happy little girls.'

In her school work Holly's teachers said she was a bright girl who enjoyed creative activities such as writing stories. According to Carr, she was especially good at English and showed her intelligence also in the way she could use the computer, mastering complex programs and sending emails and surfing the internet with ease. She also enjoyed music, playing the cornet and singing. She liked to keep up to date with the charts, and her favourite pop group was S Club Juniors.

A look through Holly's and Jessica's schoolbooks gives a poignant insight into the characters of the pair. St Andrew's Primary has four books, two belonging to each girl, used during their year in class 12 ending in July 2002. In these the two girls wrote carefully worded letters and short essays about various topics in childish but neat handwriting, printed rather than joined up. The books include illustrations which the girls coloured in themselves. Both girls wrote one schoolbook about the Victorians and another about Ancient Egypt. The first of these include letters from the girls, written to their families, about a day they spent at Wimpole Hall in

Cambridgeshire in September 2001, when they pretended to be Victorian servants.

School photographs from the outing showed Holly and her classmates wearing mob caps and Victorian clothing during the visit. Holly wrote: 'It was a brilliant day as a servant, and I am definitely going to enjoy it in the future.' Jessica, also writing in character, told how the girls had been taught to curtsy, write with dip pens, serve food, fold napkins and make beds. She wrote: 'It was really, really fun. I will like it here.' The work of both girls received praise from their teachers. The books on Ancient Egypt include pages on geography, history, the legends of the civilisation and hieroglyphics.

It is impossible to flick through the pages of these exercise books, neatly written in blue ink, without being moved. The girls' work is a picture of childhood innocence, just as their family lives were a picture of happiness and success. With Holly and Jessica doing so well at school and with their friends, with Kevin achieving increasing prosperity from his cleaning business, and with Leslie about to start a new job, the families had plenty to be happy about. On the afternoon of Sunday, 4 August 2002, nobody, not even Ian Huntley knew that these idyllic circumstances would soon be shattered and that happiness would give way to despair.

7

THE ABDUCTION

On the evening of that Sunday, both Holly and Jessica were in particularly good spirits. The two best friends had just been reunited following the Chapmans' two-week summer holiday on the Spanish island of Minorca. Jessica had returned home the previous day, looking tanned and healthy and full of exciting things to tell Holly about her stay. She had brought back a present for her friend, a necklace bearing a pendant with the word 'Love', and was dying to tell her how she'd been swimming in the warm Mediterranean and been underground in a huge limestone cavern, exploring the island with her sister Alison and their cousins Kirsty and Connor Drummond, aged 14 and 10.

Later, on day six of the hunt for the two girls, the Chapman family would release a series of moving photographs of their daughter on this holiday, pictures which were only developed after she disappeared. In one frame Jessica is seen arm in arm with Alison by the sea; in another she stretches out on a bench outside the apartment shared by the Chapmans and the Drummonds. A third charming portrait shows her sitting at the head of the table in a Minorcan restaurant, and she is also seen sitting on the floor of the cavern with the other three children. In all these pictures the lively little girl looks very happy.

Holly too had been enjoying her summer break from school. Although she had not been abroad, she had been her usual sociable self at home, using her free time to play with her many friends. As Jessica was flying back from Minorca, Holly was spending the Saturday evening with another of her favourite playmates, Natalie Parr, who was in the same class as her at St Andrew's Primary and who would sleep over at the Wellses' house that night. Natalie was later to burst into tears as she told reporters about this last day with Holly.

The classmates had been shopping with Nicola Wells in Cambridge earlier that day, and Holly had bought a CD and sweets for a midnight feast. Having set their alarm for that time, they woke to search for the sweets by the light of Holly's mobile phone before disturbing her sleeping brother Oliver and his friend in the next room. Natalie said: 'We sat up in our room and ate lots of sweets and drank Ribena. We were just talking about school. It was the best slumber party I had been to at Holly's because that night she was in a great mood and was not annoyed with her brother. Holly and Jessica are like sisters and I miss them terribly. When I heard they had gone missing I burst into tears and at times I cry myself to sleep at night.'

On the Sunday afternoon Holly and Jessica finally got the chance to get together and tell each other about all their exciting experiences of the past two weeks. The Wellses had invited their close friends Rob and Trudy Wright round to a barbecue. Later they would describe how the pair were bubbling over with pleasure at being able to talk and play with each other on Holly's computer. While the adults spent their time talking and tending the barbecue, the girls spent most of their afternoon in Holly's bedroom.

Shortly after 5pm, the girls popped out into the hallway to see how the rest of the party was getting on. They had decided to wear matching outfits: bright-red David Beckham number-seven Manchester United shirts and matching Adidas shorts, black with two white stripes down each side. They had a habit of dressing up in identical clothes, although that day Jessica had arrived at the house in an entirely different outfit and had borrowed the strip from Holly's 12-year-old brother Oliver so she could look the same as her friend. When Nicola Wells spotted the two girls in the striking red shirts she rightly thought they would make a lovely photograph together. She snapped them standing side by side, both looking straight at the camera and smiling.

Nicola had no idea that within days this picture would become the image of an innocence desecrated. The sight of Holly, with her laughing eyes and dimpled cheeks, and Jessica, with her bright, round face and upturned nose, would come to haunt the public mind over the coming weeks. The photograph would be put on missing posters in the windows of every shop and home in Soham, and in many others across the country. In a chilling stroke of chance, the two girls posed beneath the Wellses' wall clock, which clearly showed the time at four minutes past five in the afternoon. Six days into the search for the girls, the picture appeared in the *Daily Mirror* with the headline TWO HOURS LATER THEY WERE GONE. It has since emerged that they were probably dead in even less time than that. Certainly, within an hour and a half these smiling little girls would be suffering the most unspeakable ordeal.

The two girls returned to Holly's bedroom to play on her computer. A police examination of the Wellses' telephone bills later revealed that the machine had been linked up to the internet between 5.11pm and 5.32pm. The girls had sent several emails and officers spent many hours trying to find out if they had fixed up a meeting with anyone. It was thought that a paedophile could have 'groomed' them using a chatroom, but that theory proved to be unfounded. Some minutes after 5.32pm the girls decided they were bored with being in the house all day and went outside for a wander. A series of sightings and CCTV images enabled police to reconstruct this final walk.

Wander is just the right word for it, because the short, meandering route of less than half a mile suggests little sense of a fixed purpose. The pair left Holly's house in Red House Gardens and turned out of the cul-de-sac, heading towards the centre of the town. They walked slowly along a residential side street, Tanners Lane. Then they turned right into the busier main road, Sand Street, which becomes Soham High Street a few hundred yards further up. They crossed the road, walked up a small lane and across the car park of the Ross Peers Sports Centre. Here the girls were picked up at 6.13pm by CCTV cameras. The smudged images of the pair walking side by side were recovered by police and shown at a press conference the following week.

As the lonely, ghostlike figures crossed the car park they passed two men and two women coming in the opposite direction who were also filmed on CCTV leaving the sports centre. Moments after being first seen on camera, Jessica and Holly went into the building and were spotted by the duty manager there. She pressed the button to let them in through the door and they went to the vending machine in the foyer to buy some sweets. According to the sports centre's chairman, Paul Day, they had been there many times before for the same purpose.

Mr Day's assistant Claire Norton was the last person to see the girls before they fell into Huntley's clutches. She said the pair were ambling arm in arm and appeared to be without a care in the world. Minutes earlier, Mark Tuck and his wife Lucy, who were driving down Sand Street, also saw Holly and Jessica. Mark remembered saying to his wife, 'Look – there are two little Beckhams over there.'

As the two girls emerged from the alleyway called Gidney Lane, into the open expanse of the car park of Soham Village College, they found the grounds completely deserted. On a Sunday evening several weeks into the summer holiday, the area was shunned by schoolchildren and adults alike. Most of the population of Soham were sitting down to their dinner, and the area of tarmac, about 250 yards long and 30 yards wide, was devoid of cars. To the left, the neatly mown lawn leading up to the college was equally empty. The only sound was the slight breeze stirring in the leaves of the tall sycamore hedge lining the car park to the right and separating it from the ditch. Of all the peaceful places in this quiet town, this was probably the quietest.

Kevin Wells would later ponder over these moments, picturing the innocent final meanderings of the two friends. He said: 'It touched a chord in the nation's hearts because people could see that here were two beautiful young girls from loving families who were doing nothing wrong. It was a lovely summer evening, they were within their parameters, they had a mobile phone, they were together and they were taken. It's still very difficult to accept. I think people just felt it could so easily have been their daughters.'

From what we know of their movements earlier in the evening, it is likely the girls were in good spirits as they walked across the car park towards the rear entrance to the school grounds. They were probably skipping and laughing in their usual manner, and may have wandered across the lawn to throw grass clippings at each other or stopped to kick small stones across the tarmac. They were certainly in no hurry and had no particular reason to be in the area. The girls had come to the school grounds in a vague spirit of adventure, perhaps to see what the place looked like when all the children had gone home.

Their carefree mood was poles apart from the dark, troubled mentality of the man they were about to meet. Huntley, who habitually lived his life on the brink of depression, was in a particularly grim frame of mind. He resented the fact that Carr had deserted him to visit her mother in Grimsby. Fiercely jealous, he suspected she would be exposed to the company of other men and might be persuaded to cheat on him. Huntley's huge insecurities were betrayed by the way in which he tried to keep tabs on her by telephone across the weekend. Knowing Carr was going out on Saturday night, he sent her a text message late that evening demanding to know where she was.

Then, at 9.53 on Sunday morning, he tried to call her mobile. But Carr was still asleep recovering from her hangover and did not reply. She was out of his sight, beyond his control- and he hated it. All through the morning and afternoon Huntley was fuming. He tried to distract himself by renting a video from Blockbuster. Then he walked his dog past the sports centre. Finally, at 6.24pm, he got the return call from Carr. The couple spent two minutes 13 seconds engaged in a furious row, before Huntley ended the call in disgust. At 6.30pm Carr sent him a text message saying: 'Don't make me feel bad I'm with my family'. Huntley did not reply, for by this time he had found other females upon whom he could vent his power lust and hatred.

Although Holly and Jessica had not arranged any meeting, it is likely that they made their way towards the caretaker's house deliberately. Once they were in the area, it was natural enough for them to drift by the squat brick building at the far corner of the grounds from Gidney Lane, because they were always happy to see the woman they knew as Miss Carr. They had both been very disappointed that Carr, who had worked as a teaching assistant in their class at St Andrew's Primary for five months before the summer holidays began, had not been given a permanent job at their school and had been forced to leave. That is not to say that calling in at the house was a regular habit with Holly and Jessica; far from it. In fact, witnesses agree that they had never been known to visit this area alone and outside school hours before. But, as local girls, they were well aware that Carr lived in the house with her boyfriend Huntley, and they almost certainly walked past to see if she was in.

There were no witnesses to what happened next except the girls and the man who is now locked up for life for their murder. The time was 6.30pm, and it was still broad daylight when Holly and Jessica came across Huntley in the garden of his home at 5 College Close. The scene took place in an open area surrounded by possible vantage points, but nobody was there to see. The nearest neighbours lived through the school gates and around the corner in College Close proper, and the houses in the road behind the grounds, a continuation of College Close, were screened from view by trees. The home of Huntley's next-door neighbour was so completely blocked from sight that she had never set eyes on the caretaker and was not aware there was a new man in the job.

All the same, the possibility that someone had somehow spotted Huntley's encounter with the girls was to prey on his mind during the following days. The caretaker knew he could have been seen talking to them by anyone passing through the extensive grounds on this side of the school, and there was no way he could be certain that the area was totally empty. Huntley would develop a paranoid belief that he had been spotted, a belief that would eventually lead to his downfall. Because he thought someone may have seen him with Holly and Jessica, he began to fear the police were following his every move, and this fear is what prevented him from disposing of the clothes in the hangar. And because he thought there might be witnesses, he would have to admit to police that he had met the girls that evening. He would have to tell officers he was one of the last people to see them alive. Otherwise, someone else might tell them instead.

As one detective put it: 'A lot of Huntley's behaviour after he'd killed the girls seems odd until you think about the way this happened in the first place. A lot of people have asked the question: why did he bring suspicion on himself by telling everyone he was one of the last to see them alive? The answer isn't that Huntley is especially stupid – it's got more to do with the fact that he didn't plan any of this. He took them from a place that was very public in an area where he is very well known. He knew if he didn't tell us about meeting the girls and somebody else had seen him he would instantly become the prime suspect.'

Circumstances forced Huntley to tell the truth about meeting the girls outside his home at 6.30pm that evening, and officers believe he may also have told the truth about how the meeting took place. According to Huntley's testimony to the police, he had been washing his Alsatian, Sadie, in his garden when the girls walked past. Experienced detectives say this aspect of his statement has a ring of truth about it, because it refers to a very specific and quite unusual activity, not the kind of all-purpose commonplace excuse which would automatically spring to Huntley's mind. It seems likely that the girls, both of whom loved animals, stopped to pet the dog and talk to the caretaker about his girlfriend, their favourite teaching assistant.

According to the killer himself, that is exactly what happened. He would later tell reporters that they chatted to him about Miss Carr, asking how she was. In the Huntley version of events, the two girls then skipped away from his home alive and well. He added: 'I must have been one of the last people to speak to them. You can't help thinking about it.' The police would later think carefully about how Huntley knew he was one of the last people to speak to the girls. They believe that what actually happened was that Huntley, in the house on his own while Carr was away in Lincolnshire, engaged the girls in a far longer conversation. He probably joked with them in his usual friendly manner with children, and talked about their school and the good times they had had with Carr in their class. It is also likely that the fervent Manchester United fan chatted about football and the David Beckham number-seven shirts they were wearing.

Then, at some point during that conversation, a stirring within Huntley prompted him to try to lure the girls inside his house. It is unlikely he intended to kill them. Probably he got the pair inside the house using their fondness for his fiancée, telling them Carr was inside and would like to chat. It is likely he told them the same lie he later repeated to the police: that she was upstairs having a bath. We will never know for certain, but at some point around 6.30pm the front door of the caretaker's house closed behind Holly and Jessica. They would never come out again alive.

8

THE PANIC OF
THE PARENTS

Not five minutes' walk from Huntley's home, Holly's parents were winding up a long and happy Sunday gathering with their close friends Rob and Trudy Wright. The mood was light-hearted and relaxed; the couples had known each other for many years, and the talk flowed freely. The barbecue had been a resounding success, and even the intermittent rain had failed to dampen the party's spirits. Instead they had moved the equipment out of the garden and under the shelter of the garage. Then Kevin and Rob had shared a few beers while doing the cooking. Once the meal was finished, Nicola and heavily pregnant Trudy chatted in the kitchen, while the two men sipped their coffee and played cards. No-one heard Holly and Jessica leave the house. As far as the adults were concerned, they were still upstairs playing in Holly's bedroom, where they had gone after eating their dinner.

The time was approaching 8.00pm and the sky was darkening outside as the Wrights began preparing to leave. Nicola went to call the girls so they could bid goodbye to the guests.

With a growing sense of alarm, Nicola searched every room of the house. She looked in Oliver's bedroom, in her own bedroom, the bathroom, the sitting room and the kitchen. She rushed out into the garden and then out of the front door into the street. She looked left, and then right. The road was empty. Light-headed from rushing about and from the fear racing through her, she stopped for a moment to steady herself. Trembling all over, she told Kevin that something must be wrong. The couple repeated their search of the house; again they looked outside for the girls and again there was no sign of them. Maybe, they thought, Holly and Jessica would come skipping home soon after 8.30pm, the time they knew they must be at home and ready to be put to bed.

But the minutes ticked by and still no little girls in red Manchester United shirts came running around the corner. At 8.45pm Nicola picked up the phone and dialled the Chapmans' number. She didn't want to be the bearer of worrying news, and was already beginning to feel an awful weight of responsibility and guilt over the girls' absence, a weight which would soon grow into an almost intolerable burden. She told herself that they must have gone to the Chapmans'. She imagined they would probably be at that moment playing in Jessica's bedroom or outside her house in Brook Street. But the answer came back that she was dreading. Sharon Chapman said the girls weren't there.

Nicola's phone call came as a shock to Sharon. She had been enjoying a quiet Sunday evening with her family, secure in the belief that her youngest daughter was playing with her best friend a few streets away, as she had done so many times before. Immediately worried, she dialled Jessica's mobile phone. She had given her the blue Nokia 5110 handset so that she could contact her at any time and make sure she was all right. Jessica, always careful to follow her mother's advice, also had the habit of calling home of her own accord several times a day when she was out playing.

To Sharon's horror the mobile did not ring through; in place of her daughter's voice was the cold, detached tones of the recorded message: 'The Vodafone you are calling may be switched off. Please try again later.' Sharon did try again, and again, dozens of times getting the same response. It was unheard of for Jessica to turn off her phone. Sharon was in a state of panic. Thinking the girls might have gone to see another friend or a member of the family, she began a feverish ring-around of all the households she knew in Soham. She struggled to maintain her composure as she begged friends and relatives for news of the girls – to no avail.

By now Nicola and Kevin were frantic. Kevin, always a courageous, determined character, did not pause to worry over the agonising situation. Realising he was over the alcohol limit for driving, he set off on his bike to look for the girls. Holly's brother Oliver also went out on his bike to help in the search. He started with the route from Red House Gardens into the centre of Soham, the route the missing pair had, indeed, taken two hours or so earlier. From his house in Brook Street, Leslie Chapman was setting out in his car to do the same, and his wife took the couple's other car and set off in the opposite direction, her eldest daughter, Rebecca, in the passenger seat.

Kevin, Leslie and Sharon each went the length of the High Street, of Sand Street, College Road, eyes scanning every bend, every corner and every alleyway. The fathers passed each other at least twice as they travelled up, down and across the town time after time. They checked the recreation ground and the church, the supermarket car park, the Ross Peers Sports Centre. They passed several of the spots where the girls had wandered earlier that evening, but in the quiet streets devoid of people their passing had left no imprint. Kevin stopped everyone he saw to ask if they had spotted his lost daughter. The answer in each case was no.

After an hour of scouring the streets in the car, Sharon pulled up outside the Wellses' house to ask Nicola if there was anything, any possible clue, as to where the girls had gone. The two women racked their brains, but came up with nothing. The disappearance was so completely out of character that neither of them could think of an explanation, other than one which was too terrible to speak of. Sharon told Nicola: 'You know they don't do this. It is too long.' At 10pm Sharon decided to call the police.

Officers were at the Wellses' home within minutes.

Soon they too were mobilising search teams to drive and walk the streets, as Kevin and Leslie continued their own hunt. Kevin called his business partner Scott Day and asked him to drive round Soham in the van they used for work. The police asked for a list of the girls' friends, and went round to the home of each of them. Holly and Jessica's classmate Natalie Parr was woken at 2am by officers knocking on her door. She told them of dens and gardens where the pair played. But the fear that something terrible had happened was immediate. 'I thought somebody had taken them,' Natalie told me later.

At 1am phone engineers tracked the signal from Jessica's pay-as-you-go mobile phone and found it was last detected coming from the area of Soham or the surrounding countryside. At such short notice, they could not narrow its location down any further than the wide rural area covered by a mast at Burwell, near Newmarket. They also loaded extra credits on to the phone, in case Jessica had run out. The frantic hunt went on through the night, the parents becoming more and more desperate. Scott Day would later describe how Kevin shouted his daughter's name repeatedly into the darkness at the school, only to hear it echo across the foggy, empty playing fields and meet with no reply. At 6.30am the exhausted fathers had been down every road in Soham and the surrounding area many times. Shattered with anxiety and lack of sleep, they had no option but to take a rest.

Eight days later the parents were to describe these horrible moments in an interview with Colin Baker on ITV's *Tonight* programme, presented by Trevor McDonald.

They relived the disappearance of their daughters in the hope that they were still alive, and that an abductor might take pity on them if he witnessed their ordeal on television. By this time, with the hunt for the girls yielding nothing more than a series of false leads, they were desperate.

Colin Baker: When did you first realise Jessica was in trouble?
Sharon Chapman: Nicola rang me to say the girls weren't there and were they at mine? I rang her phone [Jessica's mobile] straight away, the first thing I did ... I then panicked from there onwards because I knew that wasn't like Jessica.
Leslie Chapman: That's when the alarm bells started going in both families. My wife got in one car with my eldest daughter and she went one way. I got in the other car and went the other way. I bumped into Kevin on, I think, two occasions and said: 'Right, if you're going there, I'll go here.' He was going to the sports hall, I went to the rec and all the haunts we know they go to.
SC: When I got back to Nicola's I said: 'That's it, I've got to call the police. You know they don't do this, it's too long.'
CB: When did you first think they may have been abducted?
LC: As parents you think that straight away,

not after a few hours. You think, my God, is this happening to me? You always think it's happening to someone else but it's happened to us and all we want is the children back.

CB: What warnings did you give Holly about outside dangers?

Kevin Wells: We were drumming it into them that you never talk to strangers, don't go in anybody's car or anything. I ... remember mentioning on the lines that 'you have a lot of friends and family around you but you must be aware not everyone carries that agenda'. So it has been discussed. We also did check the text messages every evening when the phone was put up for charging by the children. We go through both the phones and have a look.

CB: How did you discover they were missing?

Nicola Wells: We just assumed they'd gone upstairs to play. We shouted: 'Come and say goodbye' ... I shouted several times and then popped up ... they weren't there. I just thought perhaps they had popped outside but ... they weren't anywhere to be seen. Half-past eight is their cut-off time to come home ... I started thinking: if she's going to be late she will phone me ... At quarter to nine I phoned Jessica's mum.

CB: What did you do then?

KW: I was out all night. We searched right through until 6.30. Our fears were that the girls

were injured and one was staying with the
other ... friends and family were out. We did
the walks Holly knew, the school fields,
recreation ground, friends.

CB: When did you first think they had been
abducted?

KW: We knew they'd been taken on the Sunday
night. It was our comments to the officers that
this is an abduction – we knew ... Their
mannerisms, character, it's textbook stuff –
someone's taken them.

As these moving interviews make clear, the Wellses and
the Chapmans knew there was something very badly
wrong the moment Holly and Jessica disappeared. It was
so out of character for the two home-loving 10-year-olds to
go off without saying a word. They were both sensible girls
well versed in the rules about not talking to strangers and
not going to places where they were at risk. Yet, despite
the sickening gut feeling that their children had been
abducted, the Wellses and the Chapmans still dared to
hope. They clung desperately to the glimmer of a chance
that by some miracle their daughters were merely lost or
kidnapped but unharmed, that they would be found alive
and well. They had no means of knowing that their hopes
had already been dashed.

9

THE MURDERS

By the time the Wellses and the Chapmans began their frantic search at around 8.30pm on Sunday, 4 August, Holly and Jessica were already dead. As the families would learn two agonising weeks later, Ian Huntley had killed them soon after enticing them in through the front door of his squat little house.

Once the police found out Huntley was the murderer, they did their best to piece together exactly what had happened to the two girls. Unfortunately, their killer was so ruthless in destroying evidence that he also robbed his victims' families of much of the knowledge that forensic examinations can deliver in such cases. As one detective put it: 'Huntley was not a particularly clever murderer in several respects, but he was unusual in his awareness of forensic methods. His destruction of forensic evidence was remarkably thorough.' Because Huntley burnt the girls' bodies so carefully, it is difficult to say for sure how they were killed. Following their discovery in a ditch near Lakenheath on Saturday, 17 August 2002, Home Office pathologist Dr Nat Cary would spend many gut-wrenching hours probing these questions.

However, detectives who worked on the case believe much can be learnt about the murder using other, non-scientific methods. We know for a fact that Huntley had not planned to carry out this crime. The girls had arrived at his home by chance, and it was by chance that they were interested in talking to the caretaker because his girlfriend Carr happened to have been their teaching assistant. It was also pure chance that nobody else had passed by while Huntley was talking to the 10-year-olds from his front garden. If anyone had, then that seemingly insignificant encounter would almost certainly have saved the girls' lives. Huntley had preyed on the two friends in an entirely opportunistic manner. He had spotted them walking, alone and vulnerable, though the college grounds – there was a clear view from the garden – and his evil, sadistic nature had responded instinctively to the sight. His intentions in enticing them inside can only have been sinister, but it is likely that they were not fully formed even at the point when the two girls stepped into his home. Instead the horror unfolded spontaneously and accelerated under its own tragic compulsion.

Once the girls had agreed to enter his house, Huntley led them into the dining room. The police believe he told them Carr was upstairs and was going to come down to see them.

He had probably played on their sympathy, saying she was lying down in bed. She hadn't been feeling all that well since their school had rejected her application for a permanent job at the end of the summer term. According to the theory, Huntley waited with the girls and perhaps sat or stood next to them. His conversation became more flirtatious and maybe he pretended to try to show them something. He knew he had the girls alone and to himself in the house, that they were completely in his power.

Detectives believe he may have tempted them into drinking alcohol, or fed them squash laced with the date-rape drug GHB. He may have tried to knock them out with chloroform. But it seems he failed to make them unconscious of his twisted design.

At some point, probably only minutes after leading them into the dining room, Huntley made a grab for one of the girls. We will never know which one, or exactly how he assaulted her. But her reaction and that of her friend threw him into a rage. As one officer put it: 'Huntley liked control, he liked to have power over women – that's why he was attracted to vulnerable young girls. He put on a front of being confident and even arrogant, but underneath he had a massive sense of inadequacy, particularly when it came to the opposite sex. He couldn't handle any kind of rejection. If any woman snubbed him he went mad.'

Terrified by the friendly caretaker who had suddenly turned into a monster, the frail figures struggled to escape. Huntley is not a large man, but the elfin girls had no chance against him. In an explosion of violence, he killed them. He may have knocked at least one of them to the floor with his fists, but if so the blows were not hard enough to break any bones. Whether he hit them or not, it is thought he killed both by stopping them from breathing.

In an absurd account put forward at his trial, Huntley claimed Holly drowned in the bath while trying to stem a nose bleed, and that he accidentally killed Jessica as he tried to quieten her screaming. What he said was dismissed by the court, but given his habit of weaving half-truths with his lies, some of the suggestions may have been accurate. He probably strangled Holly first, then turned his murderous attention to the screaming Jessica. He probably murdered Jessica by holding her down and smothering her mouth and nose with his palm. The girls, fit and healthy as they were, struggled as he extinguished their lives. One of them reached out at his face with her right hand and bravely dug her nails into his cheek. She scraped three marks an inch long just above the jaw line on the left of Huntley's face, which were noticed the next day by PC Russell Goldsmith.

The police are convinced Huntley did not stab, cut or beat the girls with an object. It is doubtful he used a weapon; not having planned the attack, he probably didn't have one to hand. Again, we will never know for sure, because of the lack of forensic evidence. The painstaking care with which Huntley later cleaned the room suggests there may have been splatterings of blood.

What evidence we have suggests he killed the girls pretty quickly after he got them in the house. After they were dead he carried them upstairs and placed them on his bed, for a purpose known only to himself. From what the police have pieced together, it seems that Holly and Jessica did not suffer the ordeal of rape. But that wasn't thanks to any mercy on the part of Huntley.

The time now was around 8.30pm, just about when the girls' families were starting to worry. While the Wellses and the Chapmans were in panic over the disappearance of their children, the man responsible for their pain at this point and for the rest of their lives was himself in a state of agitation. Huntley had just murdered Holly and Jessica in a senseless, brutal and totally unplanned attack in his own home. An urge to exercise power and control had led him to lure them inside.

His horrific act was not in the conventional sense a crime of passion, but he had been in the grip of powerful emotions, overcome by hatred and fear. As his disturbed state subsided, the consequences of what he had done hit him like a heavy blow to the stomach. His past experience of being arrested for alleged rape made it very easy for him to imagine how the police would hunt him down for this. He was terrified of being caught and of going to jail for the rest of his days, and from now on his actions would be dictated by that terror.

Once Huntley's instinct of self-preservation took over, he became a changed man. From this point he would try to avoid detection in an incredibly calculated manner, taking steps to conceal evidence that would amaze detectives. There seems to have been very little that was calculated about the crime itself. Huntley's luring of the girls into his home had been purely opportunistic. But everything he did next was thoroughly planned and thought out. In the midst of a whirlpool of emotions, he was still able to narrow his thoughts down to the practical matter of removing all traces which would prove he had committed this crime. So the man who had just committed appalling acts of violence against the girls carefully bathed their corpses.

Either before or after carrying the girls to the bathroom, Huntley removed the Manchester United strips they were wearing in the happy photograph taken at 5.04pm that evening. He lowered the bodies one after the other into the water. While he was putting one of the girls into the bath, he slipped and dropped the body on the side of the tub. The impact left a crack in the rim of the bath which Huntley could not manage to rub away. Later he would explain this strange detail to the police by using his favourite excuse of washing his dog. He would tell officers that it was Sadie he had dropped, and that the impact of her body had caused the mark.

It is thought that Huntley soaped the bodies carefully and rinsed both of them several times to make sure all traces of his DNA were washed off. He then dried them and put their clothes back on, rolling the shirts back on to the tiny torsos and pulling the delicate limp arms through the sleeves. Huntley performed these tasks in the thorough manner of the good caretaker. He then began clearing the house as well, stripping the killing room of every single scrap of furniture and washing both the room and its contents from top to bottom. He worked in his usual manner, quickly and methodically, no longer showing any signs of his earlier frenzied behaviour. His actions at this point are distinguished by a remarkable calmness; he patiently scrubbed away at the house while he waited for the last light of day to fade outside.

Huntley was to continue his clean-up after he had disposed of the bodies, making sure that every corner of the three-bedroom house had been washed and polished and hoovered several times over. When I visited the house the following Thursday, it still showed the results of this deep clean. The walls, floors and surfaces were gleaming and completely free of dust. The police later revealed the room where Huntley had killed the girls had been totally stripped, and the caretaker claimed he was in the middle of redecorating it. On occasion, before he came under suspicion, when officers or journalists visited his home, Huntley tried hard to prevent them from seeing into this area of the house. Several would remember later how he had cleverly obstructed their view of the dining room with his body and directed their gaze towards the living room instead. As time went on Huntley would become confident that he had removed all forensic evidence of the murder from the premises, so much so that he would stand up in court and protest an innocence which everyone knew to be bogus.

For now, though, the problem he faced was what to do with the bodies.

10

A LONELY PLACE

Like everything else he did in the aftermath of the murders, Huntley's choice of a place to hide the remains of Holly and Jessica was logical, cool-headed and cunning. A less devious individual would have panicked after committing a crime of such magnitude and perhaps tried to flee the country. Even a relatively intelligent criminal might have been tempted to dispose of the bodies in one of the many marshes, ditches and rivers around Soham. That way the killer would have been rid of the incriminating evidence as quickly as possible – the natural desire of anyone in Huntley's situation.

But this murderer was possessed with a far greater than average degree of self-control, despite having carried out such a rash act in the first place. He knew the area would soon be swarming with police and that this crime would be of such importance that every ditch and drain for miles around would be searched. On the other hand, he realised that to travel far would attract suspicion. Any absence from home after the girls' disappearance would attract the attention of the police. If he was going to risk a journey, it had better be a short one which could easily be given an innocent explanation.

Although he was originally from Grimsby some 100 miles away, Huntley knew this area of East Anglia very well. His father had lived for five years in Littleport, along the A10 north of Ely. And in the other direction, to the east of Soham, his grandmother lived in an old people's home in Lakenheath. From time to time stories appear in the local or national press about bodies being buried in Thetford Forest. Less than a week into the hunt, my colleague Aidan McGurran, who covers East Anglia for the *Daily Mirror*, predicted the girls would be found there. And he was right. For the expanse of fens and woodland around the Norfolk town of Thetford, in fact, stretches down into the neighbouring county. The maze of mile after mile of wild scrub covers the area around Brandon, Suffolk, and at its southern tip reaches the Lakenheath airbase. Visitors to this vast wooded area rarely leave the public footpaths, partly because the marshy parts can be treacherous. Also, in the clearings and underneath the canopy of trees wherever the light penetrates, the undergrowth is impenetrable. Bracken and bramble clumps as tall as the average person deter walkers from venturing far from the established paths.

The southern edge of this wild tract of land was not only

next to where Huntley had stayed in his younger days, but was also well known to him because, as a plane spotter, he used to watch the military jets at the base. This place was only 17 miles from Soham, going there would involve only a short absence from home. Also, if anyone were to see him heading off in that direction, he had the easy excuse of going to see his grandmother, Lily Gollings, who was disabled and 80 years old and needed someone to check on her from time to time. The police later developed the theory that Huntley had visited Mrs Gollings at some time after the murders, and nine officers carried out a search of her bungalow at the old people's home. The house was two miles from the spot where Huntley dumped the bodies, and a footpath next to it leads into the woodland which he selected for that purpose.

Detectives would also search the home of Huntley's father, Kevin, because they suspected Huntley had visited the house after the murders. Nothing of interest was found on either premises. Whatever the killer's intentions regarding his relatives, it was clear that at this point his best option was to head for his old stomping ground in Suffolk and search for a suitable spot there.

By now it was past 8.30pm and daylight was giving way to a warm but drizzly summer night. Huntley wrapped the girls up in a blanket and bundled them into the back of his red, J-registration Ford Fiesta. Small as the girls were, there was not enough room in the boot itself for the two of them, so Huntley folded down the back seats of the hatchback, making sure the suspicious-looking bundle could not be seen through the rear side windows. In daylight the load could have been spotted much more easily, but it is almost impossible to see into the interior of a car as it is driving along at night.

The police believe Huntley reversed his car out of the grassed-over area that served as a drive in the gathering dusk. He passed slowly though the back gates of the college and turned right down College Road. Passing rows of modern houses on either side, most of which still had their lights on, he turned right by the library into Clay Street and carried on towards the town's war memorial, passing Saucy Meg's Café on his left. He was right in the centre of Soham, and by this time he could easily have run into the Wellses or the Chapmans who were beginning their frantic search of the town.

But no such awkward events got in the way of Huntley's mission. As was usual on a Sunday night in the tiny Cambridgeshire town, the streets were deserted. Lights illuminated the small square around the war memorial, but there was not even the group of teenagers who are often to be found lolling against the memorial on a summer's evening.

Huntley turned left at the T-junction on to Soham High Street and drove in a north-westerly direction. He continued past the post office, the supermarket and St Andrews Church on the left. He was passing through the town's main street, where he could easily have been spotted had anyone had a reason to look for him. But they didn't, and the caretaker drove by unnoticed, compelled to travel slowly through a series of sharp bends. The planners of Soham are fond of their speed calming measures, and sudden corners, large humps and other obstructions make driving above 10 miles an hour unpleasant in the town. They also add to the sense that the fenland community is one of the safest places in Britain to bring up a child.

A few hundred yards further on towards the roundabout which joins the A142 bypass, Huntley took a right turn down Great Fen Road. This narrow lane leads north out of Soham and away from any major highways or settlements. Huntley knew it well, using it regularly as a back way both to his father's home in Littleport and to his grandmother's house in Lakenheath. With very little traffic and flanked on either side by vast, flat, empty fields, the road was ideal for Huntley's purposes. With the bodies of two 10-year-olds in his boot, Huntley did not want to be seen by anyone, so he zig-zagged across the wide open fens, crossing Great Fen then turning left along the B1104 to the hamlet of Prickwillow. There he turned right, taking the B1382, another narrow, fairly straight road cutting through the flat landscape across the drain-like River Lark and the Ely to Thetford railway line. Reaching the A1101 east of Littleport, he found that this road was also devoid of traffic, passing no more than a handful of cars travelling in the opposite direction before he turned left down another tiny country lane heading into Lakenheath.

Huntley's journey so far had taken around 30 minutes, and it had brought him to perhaps the most dangerous point on his route, Lakenheath itself. The caretaker was a well-known figure in the large village. His grandmother still lived there, and he had spent a lot of time staying in the area when his father Kevin lived in Wangford Cottage in the nearby hamlet. Over the years he had been drinking in the local pubs and there were many who could have recognised his car. Skirting the village centre and heading north on the B1112 past his grandmother's house, Huntley drove steadily and within the speed limit. But under his controlled appearance was an inner state of high anxiety. Leaving the last houses of Lakenheath behind brought him a sense of escape.

A few hundred yards further and Huntley could breathe still more easily as he turned right off the main road into a lane heading through the hamlet of Wangford. The road was so narrow that Huntley had to slow down to speeds of between 20 and 30 miles an hour. Here, the farmland, with its settlements dotted around the countryside merges into the flat, wooded expanse which continues up to Thetford. Huntley passed the cottage next to the church where Kevin had once lived and to his right appeared the Lakenheath airbase. Despite its name of RAF Lakenheath, the base is in fact used by the US air force, as is nearby RAF Mildenhall. At that time of night, the site was quiet and there was little movement to be seen on the other side of the 12-foot-high wire fence. The road, which leads along the northern edge of the base to join the A1065 near Brandon, is wide enough for only one vehicle at a time. At some stage it has been surfaced, but the tarmac is broken in many places and is punctuated by large potholes. The road cuts through steep grass banks on either side and there are few passing places. If another car had driven along it in the opposite direction, the driver might well have noticed Huntley during the difficult manoeuvering needed for one vehicle to pass the other. Huntley had his heart in his mouth for fear of such an eventuality, but he pressed on.

His local knowledge, though extensive, dated back some years, and he may not have been aware of how recent world events had affected even this remote area. As a result of the attacks on the World Trade Center in New York and the Pentagon in Washington on 11 September 2001, security around all American and British military facilities had been stepped up. Like other installations at this time, less than a year after the terrorist outrage, the Lakenheath airbase was on high alert. Police and military personnel patrolled the periphery on average every hour. Huntley, driving a car not known in the area at a suspicious time of night, right next to the outer fence of the base, could easily have run across one of these patrols and been stopped. In this respect he hadn't made the brightest choice of place to bring the bodies of the two girls. But in the event he did not encounter any military or civilian police and in all other respects his hiding place was ideal.

About two miles along the lane Huntley turned on to a dirt track on the right. His Fiesta was not built for the bumps and troughs of this cutting, which is more suitable for four-wheel-drive vehicles, and the car lurched as he drove it far enough off the lane to make sure it would not be seen while he carried out the next step in his plan. At most seasons of the year there would have been a real danger of the car, which was driven only by its front wheels, getting stuck in the mud. Huntley could have been discovered at daybreak trying to dig his way out with two bodies in the boot. But again the killer had luck on his side, for the recent dry weather of high summer had turned the mud into dust and made the track passable even for his vehicle.

In pursuit of his hobby as a planespotter, Huntley had often used this same track, the crater-strewn surface of which was made from a combination of chalk, earth and concrete. It led right up to the perimeter fence of the airbase, offering a vantage point from which Huntley could watch the runways. The caretaker had kept this location a closely-guarded secret, not wanting too many plane-spotters to gather there. He thought its close proximity to the airfield might be considered a security risk, and if enough people were to make use of it the authorities would impose a clampdown and seal off the area. Five months before Holly and Jessica vanished, he let slip the secret vantage point in a conversation with fellow enthusiast Benjamin Hickling, who turned up at Soham Village College to try to drum up business for his glazing firm. Huntley told Mr Hickling he had found an area near Lakenheath which he used often. It was 'very quiet' and you were not supposed to go there. The comments confirmed what detectives suspected. From the moment he left home to dump the girls' bodies, Huntley had intended to come to this place.

The track Huntley turned into was about 800 yards in length. It was known as Common Drove and forged a route between two large flat fields, which displayed the stubbly remnants of recently harvested cereal crops. After about 600 yards it entered a small wooded area bordering onto the airbase, a copse called The Carr, which included a pheasant rearing pen. On reaching this section, Huntley brought his Fiesta to a halt.

In his headlights the killer could make out the reflection of a waterlogged ditch running alongside the track. The channel was stagnant and full of weeds, the water held in place by a sluicegate further back towards the road. The ditch at this point was five feet deep and a quarter full of water, flanked at either side by two rows of beech trees. One of these had fallen across the cutting and its branches shielded a section of it from view. Huntley got out of the car and opened the boot.

He listened for a minute to make sure there were no sounds of any other humans in the area. The night was completely still; the nearest house was a mile away and the sky was a deep black untainted by any orange tinge from street lights. The only sound was the high-pitched screech of bats hunting nocturnal insects across the fenland.

Huntley eased the bodies out of the boot onto the rough surface of the track. He then picked up the slender corpses one by one and waded through nettles up to his waist down to the bank of the ditch below. The ground was slippery, and Huntley struggled to pick his way along it. He knew the police could deduct a great deal from footprints, so he had taped plastic bin bags around his feet. These disguised the marks he made in the damp soil, but they did not make his passage any easier. As he performed a difficult balancing act on the slopes of the cutting, he snagged Jessica's hair in an overhanging twig. He wrenched her free, leaving some of her brown strands caught on the branch.

Having brought the girls' remains to the bank, he took from his pocket a pair of black-handled scissors, and by the light of a torch he cut away their clothing. He removed their David Beckham shirts, their tracksuit bottoms and their underwear. Huntley knew that any fragment of these clothes could instantly identify the girls' bodies, and he tried his best to make sure that would not happen. He attacked the garments in a frantic fashion, hacking away with sharp, heavy duty scissors as fast as possible. He sliced Jessica's 30 inch shirt from the collar down across the left shoulder to the waist, leaving it in two pieces. After making the series of ragged cuts, he ripped the shirt off from either side. He attacked Jessica's Umbro tracksuit bottoms, cutting from the waistband to the ankle quickly and clumsily, slicing chunks of material off the main fabric. Unnoticed by Huntley, zipped up in the pocket of the trousers were telling reminders of Jessica's final hours – an enamel bracelet in the shape of a dolphin and a half-eaten packet of Polos.

Huntley, interested only in getting the evidence away as quickly as possible, cut away her knickers, chopping them at each side. He yanked off her size four Nike trainers without bothering to undo the shoelaces. Turning to Holly's body, he cut from the collar of her 28 inch top down the front in a straight line to the waist, before pulling the shirt away from the back. He hacked through the front of her black padded Marks & Spencer bra and up her Reebock tracksuit bottoms from the ankle to the waist. He sliced away her white cotton briefs and pulled off her size three Nike trainers, again without unfastening the laces. In his haste, perhaps because he was so frightened of being seen, or because the light was dim, he forgot to remove the girls' necklaces. He left Holly's chain and the beads which Jessica wore around her neck.

Huntley's movements so far had been frantic; as one forensic expert put it, he acted like a medic in an emergency, removing clothes from a patient's wounds. But suddenly the pace of his activities changed. Having cut off the clothes, he carefully placed the bodies facing upwards side by side, positioning them so that they were arm in arm and crossing their legs. Why he did this is something of a mystery, for its only effect in practical terms was to waste time and increase Huntley's risk of capture. It seems his motive must have been other than pragmatic. Possibly a twisted sense of artistry drove him to make this symmetrical arrangement. Huntley, always driven by a thirst for power, perhaps found a sick gratification in designing this tableau of their deaths, placing himself in the role of the architect who could control every precise detail. It was an action which echoed the ritualistic murders enacted by serial killers, evidence for the belief held by many who worked on the Soham case that Huntley would have killed again if he had not been caught. Another motive for the design may have been a glimmer of guilt. Certainly the girls' final – seemingly peaceful – pose had little in common with their violent deaths.

Huntley had slid the girls in turn into the shallow water under the trunk of the fallen tree, leaving them partially submerged and out of sight. Having completed his mission, he again acted hurriedly, knowing if anyone saw him during these moments he was done for. He scrambled back up the slope, climbed into his Fiesta, reversed a few yards to a wider section of the track, effected a three-point turn and was gone.

So far, everything had gone according to plan for the murderer, and the journey back to Soham was to proceed in a similar fashion. Back through Lakenheath, criss-crossing the fens towards Littleport, then through Prickwillow and back into Soham. Nobody recognised him, there were no police cars. Soon after 10 pm, Huntley had completed the 40-minute drive home, and was in position at his house, ready to pretend nothing had happened.

On the way home, his mind was spinning with thoughts about his crime. Few of those were concerned with guilt for what he had done, or even with regret for the destruction of two young, innocent lives. Instead, Huntley's brain was focussed entirely on how to deal with the huge police hunt which he knew would soon be underway. His arrest for rape in 1998 had shown him how persistent officers could be with their questioning, and how such crimes brought on the full attention of the media. He knew that as caretaker of the girls' school he was unlikely to escape suspicion. For the rest of the night he would work towards calculating a strategy.

Huntley's priority on arriving home was to get rid of the clothes in his boot. He knew hiding them in the area would be dangerous; it was likely that police would subject the school and its grounds to a thorough search. He needed to destroy these incriminating fragments of cloth, and he decided to do that with fire. But in the darkness of the summer night flames would be visible far and wide, and given its unusual timing the police would easily work out that this was a bonfire of the evidence. Luckily for Huntley, he had access to a place where he could start an indoor fire. That place was the hangar, a large shed-like building made of brick and corrugated metal which he used to store equipment like lawn mowers and goal posts. Standing just across the college green from Huntley's house, it had no windows, so nobody would be able to see what the caretaker was doing inside.

Huntley took the bin bag containing the clothes over to the hangar, scanning his surroundings anxiously for signs of anyone watching. Closing the door behind him, he was filled with a paranoid fear that he had been seen. His mind was under such strain that the fear turned into a certainty, and he would later spread a smoke screen story to counter the possibility that a witness would come forward. He told a group of special constables he had seen another man in the grounds carrying a bin bag, hoping this would deflect scrutiny away from himself. Along the wall of the hangar were five large yellow bins. The third one along from the door was empty, and Huntley spilled the contents of the bin bag into it. He poured petrol over the heap of rags and set fire to them with his cigarette lighter. The result was spectacular; fierce yellow flames shot forth from the bin and singed the cobwebs on the ceiling high above. They were followed by clouds of black smoke from the artificial fibres in the shirt and tracksuit bottoms and from the plastic on the trainers.

Within seconds, the hangar was filled with a choking,

stinking fog. Huntley was not prepared for this. He had intended a fast, clean fire and instead he had a smouldering, dirty one, the effluent of which he feared would be detected at any moment. In a panic he threw water over the flames, emptying a plastic bottle of it into the bin. Inspecting his handiwork, he saw the rags and shoes were melting and oozing a black fluid but were still largely intact. Getting rid of them would need more petrol and a lot more time, but Huntley was terrified that someone would smell the smoke if he fired up the mound again. He decided to lock up the hangar instead and deal with the problem later. In the event he would never get an opportunity to rekindle the blaze, for from this point until his arrest there would be an almost constant police presence in the college grounds. The best he could manage when he found a moment to slip back into the hangar was to push a bin bag on top of the clothes to hide them.

His mission thwarted, Huntley turned his attention to the other solid evidence of his crime, Jessica's mobile phone. The lump of plastic was difficult to burn or crush, and would not rot away. He decided to take a chance and dump it in a skip which was due for emptying on the Tuesday. Soon the police would suspend the removal of all rubbish from the area, but luckily for Huntley the skip with its incriminating contents would be taken away before then. Jessica's Nokia handset would never be found.

With the clothes and the phone out of the way, Huntley's first impulse was not to retreat and hide away from the gathering forces of justice. Rather, he took his dog Sadie and went out in search of people who could see his face and give him an alibi. This he did as soon as he had finished scrubbing himself of any dirt, mud or blood he might have picked up while disposing of the bodies.

By 10.30pm Huntley was outside the Ross Peers Sports Centre a few hundred yards from his house, in time to bump into those who were locking the place up. Sports centre workers Mark Abbott and Mary Norman and her boyfriend Jonathan Watkins were in the car park when Huntley happened to pass by. As news of the girls' disappearance had already spread, Mr Abbott asked Huntley if he had seen the pair wearing their Manchester United tops. Huntley, still working out his defence, said he hadn't. He pumped the group for information. The manhunt, it seemed, was already well underway, and the trio were heading to join many of the residents of Soham in the search. This news must have given Huntley some cause for alarm. Things appeared to be moving very quickly, perhaps faster than he had expected. It was going to be a long night.

Walking from the Sports Centre back through the grounds of the college, Huntley came across people straggled across the area, all taking part in the search. He stopped to chat with several of those he encountered, and was still in the car park at 11 pm when Jessica's mother Sharon and her sister Rebecca pulled up in their vehicle. They stopped to ask Huntley whether the girls could be hidden somewhere on the premises. Confronted by his victims' family members for the first time, Huntley did not baulk. Composing himself, he replied, 'I wouldn't think so. All the college grounds have already been searched.'

Two hours later, Huntley was still patrolling this area, trying to glean every scrap of news from the people he met. It was here at 1 am that he had his first brush with the police. Seeing dog handler WPC Anna Burton approach across the lawn out of the darkness, Huntley must have feared his time had come. But he showed no signs of being rattled. He was relieved to discover WPC Burton had not arrived to arrest him, but merely wanted his help in searching the college. Could he, she asked, provide her with the keys so she could look for the girls inside the buildings? Delighted he hadn't been rumbled, Huntley replied in his most pleasant manner that he could do better than that, he would show her around himself. And so the murderer and the policewoman made a tour of the premises, looking for signs of the girls he knew were lying dead in the bottom of a ditch 17 miles away. Using the huge bunch of keys hanging from his belt, Huntley unlocked the college gates. His German Shepherd and WPC Burton's police dog bounded on ahead as the pair called for Holly and Jessica through the empty buildings and grounds.

Then, as they walked round the back of the complex WPC Burton noticed the white hangar building where Huntley had stashed the girls' clothing earlier that night. To the caretaker's terror, she asked, did he have the keys? Huntley, knowing his freedom was on a knife's edge, blurted out an on-the-spot lie. He claimed he didn't have the keys, even though they were dangling from his key ring. The falsehood was enough to earn him a reprieve for now, but once the clothes were discovered almost two weeks later it would prove fatal to his chances of escaping justice. WPC Burton banged on the doors with her fist, thanked Huntley for his help and wished him goodnight.

For Huntley, however, the night's drama was far from over. Barely was the search of the college completed when he was approached by teacher Susan Hurrell. Like the group from the Sports Centre earlier, she was eager to know whether Huntley had seen the girls. His paranoia growing by the minute with each narrow escape, the caretaker decided he would have to admit the encounter outside his house. After all, he could easily have been spotted chatting to Holly and Jessica, and if there were witnesses a denial would be instantly incriminating. He told Mrs Hurrell he had seen the two friends briefly, at about 6.50pm, and she replied that he had to report the sighting to police.

At around 4 am Huntley did just that, telling Sgt Pauline Nelson that he had seen the missing children. She noticed the caretaker seemed fresher and cleaner than any of the others who gathered to look for the girls at this late hour. It was as if Huntley had just come out of the bath; he smelled strongly of soap and aftershave. Sgt Nelson also noticed Huntley seemed reluctant to come near her. Having been told by Mrs Hurrell that he had sighted the girls, she had to shout over to him and order him to approach. Huntley, still playing for time, still trying to work out the most convincing story, was reluctant to be too specific about when and where he met the 10-year-olds, mumbling and staring at the floor. He muttered he did not think his information was important and slipped away to take refuge in his office inside the college.

But, even here, Huntley continued to be pursued by the consequences of his crime. For at 4.15am Kevin Wells, probably the last person on earth Huntley wanted to see, turned up to ask if he could search through the school grounds. Huntley managed to brazen out the meeting, but was clearly surprised that Kevin had found him. Bewildered, he asked the anxious father, who was with his two friends Rob Wright and Scott Day, how he had known he was in his office. Then, without being asked, he excused his own presence there. He said he was writing a note to a colleague saying he would be late for work the next morning because the search had kept him up all night. The explanation, Kevin said, came 'without prompting', but at the time Huntley's demeanour was convincing enough for him not to be suspicious. Of Huntley's words, this much at least was true: he would get very little sleep that night. For when police called at his house the following morning to take a statement, he was still awake and fully dressed. Detective Constables Jonathan Taylor and Andrea Warren had been sent down to interview Huntley at length because Sgt Nelson had reported his behaviour as unusual. Huntley knew the visit was coming, and he had spent the early hours working out exactly what he was going to say. He told them he was outside his home cleaning his dog when the girls walked past art around 6 pm. He said they had chatted about Maxine before heading off down College Road. He gave the officers the impression that his girlfriend had been in the house with him at the time.

It was the framework of the story Huntley would use throughout the hunt for the girls, and he managed to deliver it convincingly. But the detectives noticed he appeared highly nervous. His palms were sweating so much he had to wipe them repeatedly down the side of the chair he was sitting on. His eyes were red-rimmed and he admitted he had not slept at all. Nevertheless, he appeared very smart, very clean. His hair was wet, as if he had just got out of the shower. And as they talked to Huntley, the detectives noticed his house smelt strongly of a lemon-flavoured cleaning fluid.

Although it was raining persistently outside, some of Huntley's clothes were hanging from the washing line. DC Warren remembered: 'He asked me why he needed to make a statement and was he a suspect? He was a bit agitated – his hands got ever so clammy.' The officers wanted to know why Huntley had changed his story, having at first told the group of people outside the Ross Peers Sports Centre that he had not seen the two girls. With characteristic talent for wheedling himself out of a tight corner, Huntley applied the fruits of the night's careful plotting. He explained he had not realised the two girls being sought and the two he had seen were the same. It was only later, when somebody else told him the missing children were wearing Manchester United shirts, that he made the connection. Once more, his skill at lying had come to his rescue, and the detectives left the premises without realising they had been talking to the killer.

With the police gone, Huntley redoubled his efforts to clean away all possible forensic traces. He directed his attention to the car, which still bore tell-tale signs of his Sunday night excursion. Although he hoped that the bodies would never be found, Huntley realised that if they were, police would study the tyre marks in the dirt of Common Drove. Applying his vivid imagination to this scenario, he became terrified that detectives would turn up at his gate and begin comparing the imprints with the tread on the tyres of his Fiesta. He needed to change them, and change them fast, yet he realised such an action would itself appear suspicious. His car had been fitted with new Centaur tyres only thirteen months earlier, and since then he had only travelled about 10,000 miles in the car. The tyres were barely worn, the front two having a tread five millimetres deep and the rear two six millimetres. The legal minimum is 1.8 millimetres. Furthermore, the fact that the car had a set of perfectly good tyres was confirmed by it having passed its MoT only 25 days previously. The only solution was to change the tyres under a false identity, and this was what the ever-devious Huntley set out to do.

That Monday afternoon, the attention of the police and journalists was focussed on the first press conference to be given by the girls' families. Bravely facing the TV cameras, Leslie Chapman begged his daughter to 'please come home'. The distraught father described Jessica as 'pretty intelligent', adding, 'It is a complete mystery why she has not phoned. It is so out of character.'

While the rest of Soham looked on in sympathy, Huntley made full use of the distraction. He drove his Fiesta to Ely Tyre Services in the nearby fenland city. He paid £100 in cash for four new Sava Effecta tyres, then bribed mechanic Chris Piggott another £10 to falsify the car registration number recorded on the bill. In place of Huntley's number

J112YWR was written L788TXR, a registration which had never been issued. The cunning ruse would not be uncovered for weeks, by which time the original tyres had been destroyed.

As an habitual sex offender Huntley knew that tread marks in the mud could be as incriminating as fingerprints. He was also aware that police scientists could detect microscopic traces of the girls' presence in his boot. So he removed the factory-fitted carpet which lined it. He covered the bare metal with an old, worn piece of carpet which had never come into contact with the bodies. Then, back at home that evening, he began an intensive clean-up of both the outside and inside of the car. At the time the people of Soham were gathering after work to resume the search for the 10-year-olds. Several of them noticed Huntley scrubbing his red Fiesta with a sponge and using a vacuum cleaner on the upholstery. It was, they remarked, rather insensitive of him to be spring-cleaning his car right now. Fearing the police would come for him at any moment, Huntley couldn't wait.

The caretaker's terror of capture gave him huge amounts of energy during this period. One thing he could not do was keep still and sit at home. Instead he campaigned for his innocence like a politician in an election race. Perhaps realising that cleaning his car had left his popularity shaken, he joined in the search with renewed vigour. When I first met Huntley, on the afternoon of Monday 5 August, he was thoroughly embedded in his role. Carrying a white, freshly cut stick in his right hand, he was calling his dog Sadie to heel as she milled about on the lawn between his house and the college. It was around 6pm, and Huntley, dressed in a green waterproof coat to ward off the slight drizzle, was among the swelling party of local people going out to search for the missing girls. I heard him talking in his Lincolnshire accent with its flat vowels, and he seemed to be giving advice to others gathered on the green. Having recently arrived on the premises with a group of Fleet Street reporters, I asked one local man who Huntley was, and I was told he was helping to direct the search because he was the college caretaker and knew the area well.

According to Soham residents who joined Huntley in looking for the two girls, he was indefatigable in his efforts that night. 'We were all keyed up and doing our best, but Huntley was the keenest person there,' one said. 'He just kept going all night, not even taking a rest. He seemed desperate to find them.' That evening Huntley searched alongside 500 of the people of Soham. One of those who worked tirelessly with him was Kevin Wells.

It was after midnight before Huntley felt it safe to abandon his searching act and return home. He was exhausted, but the effort had been worthwhile. He had made several strides towards concealing his guilt. He had worked out a story which explained away his meeting with the girls on Sunday night. He had disposed of the bodies in a place where he believed they would never be found, and had faced encounters with the police, journalists and the girls' parents without betraying himself. Yet still there were difficulties, still so much more to be done. The remains of the girls' clothes were lying in a bin yards away from Huntley's house, in a hangar which any one of the dozens of police officers in the area could decide to seach at any moment. 5 College Close still wasn't completely stripped clean, and several rooms were likely to show traces of Holly and Jessica's fingerprints, hair, skin and clothing fragments. And there remained the biggest problem of all. Carr was due back from Grimsby on Wednesday. How on earth could he explain this to her?

11

THE CARING
COUPLE

The more Huntley picked over his predicament, the more he realised his prospects hinged on recruiting Carr to his cause. Sooner or later the police would establish that he had been the last to see the girls before they disappeared. A man alone in his house, who had been linked to sex crimes ... the police would work it out. The only way he could beat them was to make Carr his partner in crime and persuade her to give him an alibi.

Armed with this conviction, Huntley made two crucial phone calls on Monday August 5. At 6.56 am he rang Carr at her mother's house, waking her from a deep, drink-induced slumber. He sounded tired and cold; he said there had been an emergency in Soham, and he had been helping police search for two children who were missing. Later that day, at 4.25 pm, he called Carr again.

What Huntley had to say would come as a bolt from the blue to his fiancée. Up to now she had been making full use of her four days of freedom, going on a weekend of drinking and dancing in the company of her mother Shirley Capp and other friends. The mother and daughter duo downed pints of lager and partied the nights away, clubbing until 2 am on Saturday and Sunday.

According to Shirley, Carr would be stricken with guilt when she realised she'd been out revelling as Holly and Jessica were being kidnapped. But at the time, she was free from such troubles. She had been given a lift to Grimsby on Saturday by Huntley's parents Kevin and Lynda, and had wasted no time in getting out on the town for a binge that lasted all weekend. On Sunday she and Shirley went on a pub crawl, drinking in the Parity Bar, the Yarborough Hotel, the Exchange Fun Bar and Chicago Rock. Carr was in the mood to party; after her row with Huntley over the telephone earlier that evening, she was determined to enjoy herself. She gulped down vodka and cokes and was soon drunk.

A few hours into her session she spotted 17-year-old Mark Thomas in the Parity Bar. The six-foot-five-inch youth towered above the rest of the crowd, and Carr made straight for him. 'She couldn't keep her hands off me,' he said. 'It was amazing – she didn't care who was watching or what they thought. She certainly knew what she wanted. Her hands were all over the place and she was desperate to go to bed with me.' At first Mark tried to escape Carr's attentions, but his friends bet him £20 that he wouldn't kiss her. So he allowed her to clasp him in a passionate embrace, and Carr spent several minutes kissing him in front of her mother.

Mark eventually made it clear that he would not sleep with Carr that night, so she abandoned him for another target. Her eyes fell upon super-fit soldier Joseph Abakah, who had just returned from a tour of duty in Iraq. Joseph, 29, said: 'She deliberately caught my eye and came over to me. Straight away she said to me, "You're really lovely."' Carr said she had recently split from her boyfriend, and was free and single. She turned the conversation to the subject of tattoos. Joseph added: 'Maxine piped up, "I love tattoos, I have two, a bumblebee and a butterfly." She lifted up the sleeve on her top to show the butterfly on her left arm. Then suddenly she said she had a bumble bee on her left breast – and she just pulled down her top and showed us. Her boob fell out in front of everybody- but her mum didn't say a word. It was no accident, she knew what she was doing.'

Carr was so keen to spend the night with Joseph that she tried to stand in his way as he left the pub. She grabbed him and kissed him before he managed to escape. Later that evening Carr was spotted having sex with a man in a car park. She and Shirley went on to finish the night in the Australian theme club Walkabout, spending most of their time on the packed dance floor.

Hundreds of the inhabitants of Grimsby saw the pair that night. Carr had spent her days in an equally carefree manner, shopping with her mother and enjoying visits to her grandfather Charles Suddaby, 91, and her uncle George Suddaby in the village of Keelby where she grew up.

Huntley's revelation would put an end to all that happy activity.

Exactly what form of words he used we will never know; only he and Carr were party to that information. No doubt Huntley used all his powers of persuasion on her. It has been established that he was violent towards Carr on many occasions, beating her black and blue and terrorising her emotionally. She would tell the police how he slapped her across the face during an argument, leaving her badly bruised. She said he did it 'to shut her up', and he would get angry even about running out of muesli.

However, her behaviour before and after the couple's arrest does not support the theory that she was coerced into lying for him. If she had been frightened for her life, there were plenty of opportunities for her to slip away during the times when Huntley was out helping the police. The huge numbers of officers in the area surrounding her home offered her the perfect protection if she had wanted it. All she needed to have done was run out of the house and into the arms of dozens of policemen who would have prevented Huntley from harming her. And at this moment, there was no way he could physically force her to support him. She was more than 100 miles away on the other end of a telephone.

Following the couple's arrest, Carr initially showed no signs of being put off her lover. She wrote to him repeatedly during the first weeks of their imprisonment, expressing sympathy over the supposed breakdown which had landed Huntley in the relatively comfortable surroundings of Rampton secure hospital. Months later, when Huntley was locked away in Woodhill prison, Carr was still sending him cards, which he put up in his cell. The key to Carr's devoted support seems to be that her extreme reliance on him, her severe insecurity without him, led her to back him up whatever the circumstances.

According to Carr, Huntley was in tears when she answered his call at her grandfather's house. He begged her to come back to Soham and help him. She said: 'It was in the afternoon, it was twenty-five past four, I was up my grandad's. That was when he wanted me to come home. He said that there were some kids who had gone missing and I said, "Oh, yeah," and he told me who they were and he said, "But the thing is, Maxine, they came in our house."'

Carr told of the conversation in a phone call to Huntley's mother Lynda while on remand at Holloway prison. She said Huntley told her Holly had a nosebleed. The little girl went to the bathroom to try to stop the flow of blood, while Jessica went into the bedroom. Through his tears, Huntley added: 'They went up and I went up. There was nowhere for her (Jessica) to sit so she sat on the edge of our bed.' Carr recalled, 'He was not talking in complete sentences. He just said he wished I had been there. He wished I was home. He seemed to find it hard to cope.'

He told Carr the police were bound to suspect him because of the rape allegation which had been made against him. She revealed: 'He said, "I am going to get fitted up again just like I did before." He was in absolute tears.'

Carr promised that she would come home and help him. They arranged for him to drive up to Grimsby the following day and collect her. Huntley was left in suspense;

he did not yet know whether Carr was going to lie for him. But his pleas for help, his tearful pledges of undying love, had been received remarkably well in the circumstances. After the conversation was over, he felt a weight lift from his shoulders, and was able to rejoin the search for the missing girls with renewed confidence.

Carr's reaction following the call was very different. Although she was only beginning to realise it, Huntley had just ruined her life. For the rest of the day she cried, overcome by shock and self pity. She told her mother she was upset about the disappearance of Holly and Jessica, because she cared for the girls so much. Shirley said, 'I remember Maxine saying they were lovely lasses, beautiful girls. She kept flicking through the TV channels looking for news about them. She was crying and couldn't eat anything.' In reality Carr cried for herself and her lover. Her actions would show she spared the girls and their families barely a thought.

The next day Huntley was speeding north up the A1 to collect her. He called in the morning to say he was already on his way. At 12.25 pm on Tuesday 6 August Huntley pulled up outside the home of his intended mother-in-law. Shirley noticed he seemed flustered and hurried, though this was not unusual with Huntley. He asked for a cup of tea and a bag of crisps. Then he helped Carr carry her belongings to the Fiesta. By chance, Shirley's neighbour Marion Clift was coming home and saw the couple standing next to their car. The boot which had contained the girls' bodies was open. Mrs Clift said: 'Maxine was with somebody – it was Ian. They were looking into the boot of the car. Maxine was crying. Ian was pale and shaking – he didn't look very well at all.' Mrs Clift's gate squeaked as she opened it, and the couple noticed her. She added, 'They both stared at me and Ian slammed the boot shut. Maxine just looked. I could see the tears. She put her head down.'

Huntley and Carr regained their composure sufficiently well to give Shirley a lift to work. Having dropped her off, they picked up hitch-hiker Robert Jeynes as they headed away from Grimsby on the A16. The couple chatted to Mr Jeynes, telling him they were from Soham, the town where the two little girls had gone missing. Huntley said he had been the last person to see the girls alive, and Mr Jeynes warned him not to say such things, adding, 'It's always the last one who sees them alive that gets done.' Huntley then mentioned how another witness, Tina Marie Easey, had come forward. He said she had 'supposedly' seen the girls after him.

After they dropped Mr Jeynes, Huntley returned to the subject of how he needed help. With the car travelling at speed and Huntley at the wheel, Carr could not get out or change her direction. She was a helpless, captive listener. Later, when she did have a choice, she would remain equally passive in the face of Huntley's evil, as if she were still locked in the car with him at the wheel. It was, he insisted, essential that she helped him. He needed her to back up his story, or else he was done for. He would be back in prison; it would drive him to a nervous breakdown, he didn't think he could survive it.

In the late afternoon they arrived home. Carr entered the property, which was full of the telltale stink of disinfectant, with foreboding. She noticed signs that something had gone very amiss. The dining room table was not in its normal place and the light fitting above it had been pulled down from its socket with all the wires showing. The carpet was wet, as if there had been a flood. In the kitchen the bedclothes and a bathroom mat were stuffed into the washing machine, which Huntley had never used before. Upstairs a crack had appeared in the white plastic bath, on the inside near the handle.

Surrounded by the wreckage of the murders, the couple discussed what to do next. Carr recalled: 'Ian just wouldn't sit still. He was pacing up and down like he was really fretting about it. He kept saying he thought he was a suspect. He said, "Oh God, if I was the last person to see them, they're going to come after me." I was scared and I agreed with what he said because I wanted it to be all right. I never really thought about the girls at that time. They were out of the equation. It was Ian, his job and his reputation.'

Together in the house where Holly and Jessica had met with their deaths, they formulated a story which would put the girls' parents through 10 more days of torment. They decided they would brazen out the manhunt. Between them they would play the part of the caring couple.

Like an acting coach, Huntley took Carr through the story again and again in minute detail. He asked her how she would respond if the police asked her this question, or that question. He wrote a crib sheet for her so she would not forget her lessons. Scrawled in Huntley's handwriting, it read:

4.55 – 5 pm got into bath approx. 5.40 – 5.45pm dog home approx. 6.15pm girls 6.25pm came down to put tea on.

That night, and on every night until their arrest, the couple would sleep in the same bed. During the days, Carr spent hours scrubbing the house, cleaning it so thoroughly that every one of the girls' fingerprints would be wiped away, along with every tiny speck of hair or skin or anything else which could yield a sample of DNA. She washed everything, even down to the dining room curtains. In her breaks she swotted up her alibi.

After three days of rehearsals, Carr got the chance to perform her act for a police audience. On Friday August 9, Sgt Mathew Johnson arrived at the caretaker's cottage on his way around Soham carrying out house-to-house enquiries. The couple let him in after making sure he was not a member of the press. Chatting to Carr informally, Sgt Johnson asked what she was wearing when the girls came to her house. He remembered: 'She laughed and made a joke that she was wearing nothing because she was in the bath.' Carr then began to banter with Huntley over whether or not she had a scar in front of her left ear. She told the officer: 'Don't put my hair colour down as ginger.' In the midst of the jokes, Carr supported her boyfriend's alibi in every detail. If only she hadn't been in the bath that evening, she said, maybe she would have talked to the girls and found out where they were going. Sgt Johnson remarked that the couple seemed 'perfectly relaxed' and were 'very co-operative'.

The next day, Carr managed to put on an equally convincing display for two more police officers, Detective

Constables Michele Hope and Stephen Long. They arrived with the dual purpose of taking a formal statement from Carr and a DNA sample from Huntley. To the guilty couple this must have been a troubling development, but Carr in particular showed no signs of being perturbed. She told DC Hope she'd had a heavy period the previous Sunday, and was having a bath to 'ease the pain'. She said Huntley had come upstairs to tell her two girls, one blonde and one dark haired, had been asking after her. Both of them had been wearing Manchester United shirts. Carr said: 'I thought it was nice that the girls had asked after me but didn't work out who they were.' DC Hope was struck by how well Carr remembered everything. She said, 'Whatever I asked her she was very clear on.'

After her arrest Carr would reveal how she screwed up courage to tell these falsehoods. She said: 'Ian wouldn't have me saying anything. We were so upset and then when the police officer came round, the lady, she took me into another room. Then I just gulped. All the details Ian told me I told them.'

Huntley, meanwhile, had managed a slightly less polished performance with DC Hope's male colleague. When DC Long handed him the consent form for the DNA mouth swab, he studied it carefully. He then became reluctant to sign it because the form said the results would be placed on a national database. Eventually Huntley was persuaded to take the test, but then asked a question which struck DC Long as strange. 'How long does DNA last?' he wanted to know.

Huntley's tuition of Carr had worked brilliantly. She

seemed not only at ease but in her element when lying to police officers. But his worries about DNA reflected anxieties about other aspects of his cover-up. For reasons known only to himself, he feared samples of his DNA were on the girls' bodies. Earlier in the week, on Wednesday August 7, he had also pestered police officers about genetic testing. That afternoon he approached Special Constables Michael Kerr and Nicola Peacock. He asked them, what did police need to make a DNA profile? PC Kerr replied that hair, skin or saliva would do. He added a single hair would be enough. Later, at around 7 pm, Huntley approached Special Constable Sharon Gilbert with similar queries. He asked her how long DNA evidence could be used. Her reply was not reassuring. She recalled: 'I said they've used it on woolly mammoths and they have used it on the Tsar's family, and I didn't think there was any time limit.'

This was not what Huntley wanted to hear. He had dumped the girls' bodies in a secluded spot where he hoped they would decay in the summer heat. He had thought that this natural destruction of the evidence would be enough to obliterate any trace of the person who had left them there. Now he knew that if he had left a DNA trace it that could be picked up for many years to come. It was a prospect so terrifying that Huntley decided to fix the problem forthwith. He jumped in his Fiesta and made his way back to the lonely place where he had left the bodies of the two girls.

It was a quiet and misty evening. Huntley arrived at the spot near the edge of the Lakenheath airbase but this time there were no bodies in his boot; instead, he had brought a red petrol can normally used to fuel the lawnmowers he used as a caretaker. He had made sure the can was full. Huntley, a smoker of Golden Virginia roll-ups, also carried with him his usual cigarette lighter. Leaving his car tucked away on the edge of the copse, he approached the section of ditch where he had left the girls' remains, making a new path through the waist-high nettles. To his horror, Huntley found somebody had opened the sluicegate further along the ditch, and the water, which had been up to two feet deep, had for the most part drained away. The bodies, though concealed under a tree trunk where he had left them, were now visible to anybody who came close enough to peer under the branches. He could make out the features of the girls and see their pale figures.

For a moment, Huntley was gripped by a terror that the corpses had already been found and he had walked into a trap. As he glanced about him into the undergrowth, he was relieved to see no signs that anyone else had been to this place since Sunday night. Apart from the track through the nettles he had just made, and the other he had made on previous occasion, the thick vegetation was undisturbed. Huntley stooped over the figures, stretched out in the bottom of the cutting where he had left them. Picking up the red petrol can, he emptied the whole contents of it over the corpses, letting the strong smelling liquid gush out over their heads, upper bodies, legs and feet. He lit the fuel with his cigarette lighter and watched it leap into flame. The pyre cannot have been a pleasant spectacle, even for a man as callous as Huntley. When the bodies were found by Keith

Pryer 10 days later, the girls' skin and flesh had been incinerated. Only parts of their backs had escaped the flames, as these areas were protected by being in contact with the damp earth. The police believe Huntley stood at the spot for only a few minutes, just long enough to see that the fire was underway. He watched as the flames died down quickly and were replaced by a slow smouldering, giving off a putrid smoke. Few would have been able to witness this macabre bonfire without vomiting.

With the fumes pouring from under the branches of the beech trees, Huntley searched the area carefully one last time to make sure he had left nothing behind. Then, taking the petrol can with him, he scaled the bank, got back in his car and reversed down to the space where he could make a three-point turn and be on his way. Less than 10 minutes later, he turned up at the home of his grandmother, Lily Gollings, in a complex of old people's bungalows known as Quayside. In Huntley's mind, turning up there was the obvious way to give himself an alibi for being in this area. This cynical use of his elderly relative was typical of a nature which was barely capable of understanding anyone's interests other than his own. His clothes stinking of the burning flesh of murdered children, Huntley exchanged a few pleasantries with Mrs Gollings before ringing Carr on her mobile. It seems he wanted to tell her he would be home for supper. Sure enough, on the way out, Huntley was seen by a neighbour. He had his alibi, which in days to come would mean the police having to subject Mrs Gollings's house to an intensive search.

The use of information gathered from police and the

press to plug the holes in Huntley's cover-up was an important feature of his behaviour during this period. On occasions his efforts backfired, as when he asked BBC journalist Debbie Tubby 'Have they found the girls' clothes?' She reported him to police for this suspicious remark. The day before he was taken into questioning, he asked one of the men leading the investigation, Detective Chief Superintendent Andy Hebb, how the abductor could access a message police had left on Jessica's mobile phone if he had thrown the handset away. Since Huntley was by this time under serious suspicion, DCI Hebb noted his remarks with interest.

Most of the time, though, Huntley was able to use his position at the heart of the action to his advantage. The daily media briefings were being held at Soham Village College and, as caretaker, Huntley was entitled to be there. It didn't trouble him to watch the parents of the girls he had murdered braving the world's media. On the morning of Wednesday August 7 he skulked behind the rows of reporters and TV cameras as police were forced to admit that they were dealing with an abduction. Sharon Chapman begged Holly and Jessica's kidnapper: 'Please give them back. We are empty without them.' One man in that room knew her pleas were in vain, but during the course of the press conference he did not utter a word. Both the Wellses and the Chapmans were in tears and clung onto each other for support. Everyone there suffered with them – except for Huntley

As the conference concluded, the killer even had the gall to approach Kevin Wells to offer his condolences. Holly's

Holly and Jessica together. *Above*:
A picture that has become tragically
familiar to the British public and,
below left, the girls with Holly's cousin.

Below right: The picture that came to
symbolise the case. The clock shows
that within two hours of the picture
being taken, the girls were dead.

Above: Jessica with her family. *Left*, with sisters Rebecca (*centre*) and Alison (*seated*) and, *right*, on holiday with her cousins and sister Alison (*centre*). Tragically, the holiday snaps were developed after Jessica's disappearance.

Below: Jessica was more of a tomboy than her friend Holly and loved sports.

Above and below left: Holly on holiday in Majorca in 2001.

Below right: Holly attended the Fenland Majorettes. In August 2002, two of her friends from the Majorettes left touching messages attached to a baton at the church in Soham.

This picture of Ian Huntley was taken before his arrest, as he played the part of the concerned caretaker.

Inset: The boy who became a monster. At school, Huntley was teased and bullied.

Maxine Carr, appealing for the safe return of Holly and Jessica. She is pictured with the card made for her by Holly on the last day of term.

Above: (*From left to right*): Nicola and Kevin Wells, Sharon and Leslie Chapman, outside the Old Bailey in April 2003.

Below: The Soham Rose, created in memory of Holly and Jessica. The aim of its creators was to raise money to serve local community needs in ways that recognised the tragedy of the girls' deaths.

This was the first picture of Maxine Carr inside Holloway Prison, taken after she had been charged.

Due to the huge publicity surrounding the trial, Stephen Coward QC, Ian Huntley's barrister (*above left*), and Richard Latham QC, for the Crown (*above right*), became familiar figures.

Below: Maximum security vans containing Huntley and Carr leave the Old Bailey at the end of one of the days in the lengthy trial.

father was on his way out of the building with family liaison officer Chris Mead when Huntley sidled up to him. Kevin said: 'I can remember having to break off my conversation because I was aware of somebody standing just behind my left shoulder – certainly too close for comfort and invading my personal space. I turned round and saw it was Ian Huntley. I said, "Hello Ian." Ian replied, "Kevin, I am so sorry. I didn't realise it was your daughter." I said, "I know. Thank you for your kind words. It just beggars belief doesn't it?" He agreed and replied, "Yes, I know."'

Whether some shred of honesty in Huntley led him to this apology we will never find out. Given the rest of his behaviour at this time and during the course of his life, that would seem unlikely. A more plausible explanation was that it lent credibility to his act. He was the conscientious, concerned character who felt the pain of his fellow human being. And to add further to this image, he went on to tell Mr Mead he wanted to make some minor changes to the times set out in his statement, having gone over the events of Sunday night once more with the help of his girlfriend. The impression of sincere distress Huntley managed to create seemed to disarm the suspicious minds of the police officers around him. Minutes later, DC Jonathan Taylor, who had taken Huntley's first statement, spotted the caretaker standing in the school hall where the press conference had just ended. Realising he had forgotten to give Huntley a consent form agreeing to the search of his house, he took the killer to one side. He explained that Huntley needed to fill out the document, which was a formality in circumstances where all the college premises were being searched. Huntley's response was dramatic. DC Taylor recalled: 'He said, "You think I have done it. I was the last person to see them or speak to them." Then he started to cry. I told him not to persecute himself and to pull himself together. I told him other people had seen the girls ... That seemed to cheer him up a bit.'

In hindsight, the outpouring of emotion would seem the product of guilt, but Huntley played the caring individual so well that DC Taylor was inclined, like many others, to put his behaviour down to excess sensitivity.

Seeing how well this tactic worked, Huntley made the admission that he had been the last to see the girls part of his act, mustering tears on a number of occasions as he spoke of his accidental link with their final movements. He blubbed away in front of detectives and journalists and TV crews, getting deeper and deeper into the part. Buoyed up by Carr's unwavering loyalty, Huntley persisted in his role and became more proficient at the deceit with the passing of time. Retracing his movements over the 13 days between the girls' disappearance and his arrest, it is evident that he actually grew in confidence while maintaining his front. Making his first statements to the police he seemed convincing enough, but afterwards, under the spotlight of the media, Huntley betrayed jangled nerves. When his sighting of the girls came to the attention of the press on Thursday, 8 August, he talked reluctantly, repeatedly breaking down in tears. At first he refused to have his photograph taken and didn't want to appear on TV. We now know this was because he was terrified that people back in Grimsby would recognise him and notify the police of his past.

Even at the time, several journalists thought this behaviour was suspicious. Press Association East Anglia district reporter Brian Farmer immediately told the police he thought Huntley was their man. My *Daily Mirror* colleague Harry Arnold, a veteran of 41 years on Fleet Street, had arrived earlier that day. When I told him of the caretaker's behaviour, Harry's response came back without a pause: 'He did it then, didn't he.' What clinched Huntley's guilt in Harry's eyes was his statement to reporters at his house.

These were the killer's words: 'I was outside cleaning the dog. These two girls Jessica and Holly stopped outside. They asked me, "How's Miss Carr?" I said, "She's not very good, she didn't get the job." I just saw them for a few minutes – I don't know where they came from. I was kneeling down washing the dog when they just appeared. They went off over towards the library. They were as happy as Larry. I've never seen them walking past this way before. They haven't run away, they didn't have a care in the world. I must have been one of the last people to speak to them – I can't help thinking about it [*tears*]. I've been with the police every single night co-ordinating the search of the college. I've been with the Essex police unit helping them. It seems they have just disappeared off the face of the earth. How can two girls go missing in broad daylight without anything, no sightings, no nothing? It beggars belief.'

Somehow, Huntley was totally certain the girls had not run away; he stated this as fact. But what Harry and others thought particularly striking was another of his certainties: that he must have been one of the last people to speak to them. In the confusion of that time, when the police were piecing together conflicting sightings from several people, how could Huntley have known that?

Earlier that Thursday, he had again sat through the morning press conference, watching CCTV footage the police had discovered which showed Holly and Jessica shortly before they disappeared. Along with the rest of the crowd, Huntley viewed the smudged frames as they flickered jerkily across the screen. He had helped set up the video equipment and seemed to watch the film taken from the security camera at the nearby Ross Peers Sports Centre with interest.

Because Huntley at first did not want to have his picture taken, enterprising photographers snatched a frame or two of him without his knowledge. They needed a picture to go with the quotes he had given reporters. These shots were later rendered unnecessary when Huntley finally decided to pose in the grounds of the college, but later still they regained their significance. For by chance the pictures showed him sitting in the driver's seat of his Fiesta chewing his fingernails. Unaware that he was being watched, his expression was one of high anxiety as he sat sideways in the seat with his legs jutting out of the open door. Above his head in the picture was a poster appealing for information about the missing girls which Huntley had stuck to the window of his house.

By this point, four days into the hunt, Carr had also got involved in the public display of innocence and was giving interviews to the media. Like Huntley, she coped astonishingly well with the part she had chosen to play, the concerned teacher distraught at the disappearance of her favourite pupils. With Carr backing him all the way, Huntley continued to participate in the hunt for Holly and Jessica as much as he possibly could. The police and media were basing themselves in the grounds of the college and holding daily meetings in the assembly hall. Huntley attended all of them, being extremely helpful to everybody concerned.

Along with others following events, I saw him and chatted to him virtually every day from the beginning of the search to the day of his arrest. He became a useful source of early information on what the police were planning to do next; he pointed us in the direction of extra power points and lavatories; he brought us chairs and opened up the doors every morning. On Friday, 9 August he stood in the assembly hall as Detective Superintendent David Hankins pleaded with the abductor to come forward. The following day he was among a crowd of local people who watched two child actors dressed in David Beckham shirts retrace the final movements of the missing girls. The reconstruction, which took place amid an eerie silence as the crowd ceased its chatter in respect, was a moving sight. But seeing the Holly and Jessica doubles walk slowly towards a fate only he knew about didn't move Huntley.

On Sunday, 11 August Huntley listened in the hall as the police announced they would interview every known sex offender in the surrounding three counties. Huntley wasn't on the Sex Offenders Register, so he knew the questioning of 700 people would be in vain.

The killer's confidence was growing as each day ticked past and he remained in the clear. An extraordinary episode on Wednesday, 14 August shows how far he had come to revel in his role. Detective Superintendent David Beck, who was leading the investigation at this point, had recorded a video appeal addressed directly to the abductor, asking him to call him in person by midnight that night. He also asked him to pick up text messages left on Jessica's mobile phone, the intention being to entice the kidnapper to switch on the phone and leave an electronic trace of his location. The 30-second tape was given out to the media at Soham Village College in the afternoon, just before the London *Evening Standard*'s deadline. The newspaper's reporter Harriet Arkell was in desperate need of somewhere to watch the tape, so she knocked on the front door of the nearest house she could find, which proved to be Huntley's.

She later described the encounter: 'Huntley answered the door and I explained that I had an unusual request to make. "I've got a copy of the video with a police appeal to the girls' abductor to get in touch, and I'm desperate to watch it in a hurry," I said. Huntley paused, looking unsure, and studied me for a few seconds. "Please," I begged. "It's an appeal for the abductor to get in touch – it may help get the girls back safe and well." "OK," he said, slowly opening the door to let me in. "But let me check with my girlfriend first." This seemed odd for such a small request, but I nodded and waited as he poked his head into the next-door room and explained that a journalist wanted to watch a video. She agreed, and he pointed in the direction of the sitting room, inviting me and Press Association reporter Sam Greenhill to go in front of him.

'The sitting room was decorated in pale pastel shades and seemed empty of personal knick-knacks, as if they had recently moved in. Huntley gestured for me to sit on the sofa while he and Carr squatted on the carpet, and took the video to put it into the machine. "Do you know we are actually getting a DVD," he laughed, "but not for a couple of weeks. You're lucky." Carr spoke for the first time. "Are we allowed to watch this?" she asked quietly. We told her she was, although it was embargoed from the national media until 6pm. Mr Beck's serious face appeared on screen and he began to speak. "I appeal to you again to work with me to stop this getting any worse than it is. You do have a way out," he said. The video lasted less than a minute, during which I and the other reporter scribbled in our notebooks and Huntley and Carr gazed at the screen, emotionless and silent.

'When it had finished we began comparing shorthand notes to make sure we both had it right. "Shall I rewind and play it again, so you can make sure you've got it all?" Huntley asked. "No, don't worry," I said. "We're in such a rush and anyway it's so short, I'm sure we've got it all down." He persisted. "No really, why don't I rewind? It won't take long.' We agreed. Huntley rewound the video and we all sat watching it again, silent apart from when Huntley shook his head and murmured: "It beggars belief."

'As we watched the video for a second time, I glanced over at the couple. If they were the people Mr Beck's video appeal was directed at, you would never have guessed. Not a flicker of emotion passed across either of their grey, pallid faces. They just looked, like most people in Soham,

173

exhausted and concerned. At the end we thanked the couple, took the video and apologised for bothering them as we raced out of the door. "It's no trouble," Huntley told me. "Anything to help get those two little girls back."'

By this stage it seems Huntley was convinced he had hoodwinked everybody. Put on the spot by Harriet's request, he responded not with hostility or even reluctance. As usual, he bent over backwards to be helpful and to get involved, acting his part out far more than was necessary and showing a relish for the role he was performing. During this period of increased confidence, Huntley would rarely restrict himself to the backstage, instead pushing into the limelight at every opportunity and becoming a kind of spokesman for the people of the town. TV crews used him as what they term a talking head, placing him in the same authoritative position as other Soham figures, like the vicar, the Reverend Tim Alban Jones.

Carr also showed a remarkable ability to act out the cover-up. Her appearances before the media gave away only the slightest hints of her guilt. One such hint came in the following interview with Sky News reporter Jeremy Thompson, recorded on Thursday, 15 August, the day before she and Huntley were taken in for questioning.

> JT: You knew the little girls – what were they
> like? Tell us about them.
> MC: Lovely, really bubbly girls, ever so funny,
> brilliant, kind towards everybody, they
> wouldn't say a bad word about anybody, they

love their families and everything, which is
why nobody believes they would ever run
away. They was very close to, um, all their
family.

JT: Tell us something about this card you are
holding.

MC: This is something I will probably keep for
the rest of my life, I think. It's what Holly gave
me on the last day of term. She was very, very
upset because I didn't get my job and she just
gave me this with a poem on the inside, saying
to a special teaching assistant really, saying
we'll miss her a lot and see her in the future.
And that's the kind of girl she was ... she was
lovely, really lovely.

Speaking to millions of TV viewers in footage which would
be repeated in bulletin after bulletin during the coming
days, Carr appeared to struggle to keep her composure, to
be on the verge of bursting into tears. Her words do not
seem greatly different in content from those of head
teacher Geoff Fisher or class 12 teacher Joy Pederson, both
of whom made similar appeals for the return of the girls.
But there is one difference in the way Carr talks about
Holly and Jessica – she speaks of them in the past tense:
'They was very close to, um, all their family.' And she says
Holly '*was* lovely, really lovely', not that she still is. Few of
the other witnesses who spoke out ventured to express
such a certainty that the girls were no more. How could
Carr know Holly's character was a thing of the past? There

was only one explanation for her slip of the tongue.

While recording another TV interview, this time for *BBC Look East*, Carr was so persistent in referring to Holly and Jessica in the past tense that reporter Rachel Dane had to make her answer the questions again, using the present tense. When the cameras rolled, Carr stuck to instructions for a few sentences then once more slipped into talking about the girls as if their lives were definitely over. Realising her mistake, she bit her lip.

The police would be poring over the exact wording of these interviews the moment it went out on Thursday, 15 August, just as they would examine all the other statements made by the couple. For by this point, despite their arrogant front, Huntley and Carr had become the prime suspects in the case. One of the reasons for this was a by-product of their high profile in the media. For people back in Grimsby who were watching Carr perform on TV were struck by an odd anomaly in her story. She was claiming to have been in Soham having a bath while Huntley chatted to the girls downstairs, whereas, in fact, they had seen her wandering the streets of her home town during that very same period on Sunday, 4 August. At least one of those who noticed this strange error rang the Cambridgeshire Constabulary's hotline and notified them of it.

With hindsight it seems it was only a matter of time before Carr's cover was blown and Huntley's alibi demolished. But the couple themselves did not waver in the face of such a possibility. On that Thursday, soon after Carr chatted to the man from Sky TV, Huntley was setting up chairs in the assembly hall of Soham Village College ready for a meeting between the residents of the town and representatives of the police. He was to stand through the meeting and listen dutifully as the police told the people of the town to look on their neighbours with suspicion. Carried away with the thought that his act was working, Huntley did not realise the meeting had been set up specifically to heap pressure on him.

The following morning he was still giving TV interviews, this time to GMTV. Wearing his trademark short-sleeved polo shirt, he volunteered to be a spokesman for the community about how Soham was feeling after their meeting the previous day with the much-criticised police. Huntley said: 'Overall I think they are coping quite well. The overall view seems to be that while there's no news there's still a glimmer of hope and I'd go along with that. I think the meeting gave people a chance to vent their frustrations towards the police. I don't think it's so much a case that frustrations are aimed at the police, it's just that there is nowhere else to aim them.' At the end of his interview, he was asked if he still had hope for the girls. He paused, then replied: 'Yes. Yes.' There were more tears as he again reflected on his brief encounter with the girls, berating himself for not delaying them for a while longer so they would now be safe. He felt 'gutted', he said. 'I keep reliving that conversation and thinking perhaps something different could've been said, perhaps kept them here a little longer and maybe changed events.'

After chatting away to the GMTV crew, Huntley went back into the hall to get ready for yet another press conference given by the parents. With remarkable courage, they had agreed to appear before the cameras 13 days into the hunt, when it was almost certain that their girls were dead. Kevin and Nicola and Leslie and Sharon looked totally shattered as they wept in front of the cameras, holding on to each other for support. Their sunken faces told of nights without sleep. Watching them silently was Huntley, still standing at the back of the press pack. He listened to Sharon describe how the days since Holly and Jessica's disappearance had blended into a blur. 'The time doesn't mean anything any more,' she said, speaking in a deadpan voice stripped of emotion. 'It just rolls into one, the hours and the days. Before you know it it's dark again. You don't realise the day has gone some days. The noise level in my house – it's so quiet, so quiet. Even though there's lots of people going in and out, in and out, it's so quiet, so empty.' The words were calculated to melt the hardest of hearts, but they didn't touch Huntley.

At around 11am on that day, Friday, 16 August, I encountered Huntley for the last time before his arrest. The college, where the press had been based throughout the hunt, had been closed to them, for reasons which would soon be revealed. However, I had left my mobile phone charger inside the hall, and so slipped in past the 'No Press' sign to recover it. Turning the corner of the corridor, I ran straight into Huntley. I thought he would throw me out because I wasn't supposed to be there, but instead he looked startled and worried by my being there and tried to slink out of my way. I started to explain my presence and the previously friendly and talkative caretaker merely mumbled something inaudible and walked off. He appeared exhausted, with deep lines across his forehead and bags under his eyes. With hindsight it seems the pressure was finally getting to him.

But still I did not suspect that at 3.45pm that afternoon he and Carr would be on their way to a police station to be questioned about a double murder.

12

INSIDE THE HOUSE
OF HORRORS

The hundreds of police officers and journalists who swarmed round the grounds of Soham Village College in the days following the girls' disappearance paid little attention to the small, detached brick building in the corner of the school's green. The modern brick house on the right as you drove into the grounds from the rear entrance looked unremarkable enough. Partially screened from the single-lane gateway by an evergreen hedge, it was easy to miss the place altogether, and those who did notice the building would not have paid it a second glance. The fluted, dark-red roof tiles and the beige brickwork were more commonly found in suburbia than here in the Cambridgeshire countryside, and the white window frames, lace curtains and white front door suggested nothing in the least sinister.

The front garden was crowded with small trees and bushes, which helped to hide the three-bedroomed property. The lawn was overgrown at the edges and around the bases of the trees, and this added to the air of shabbiness which pervaded the place. A path of concrete paving stones led up to the doorway and along the front of the building to the left, towards the nearest corner of the college complex. Like everything else about the house, the flagstones were functional rather than in any way decorative.

Behind the hedge was a drive which was really no more than a grass verge, and for most of the time a red, J-registration Ford Fiesta was parked there. A functional, economical car to go with a functional, sensible home – the scene suggested completely unremarkable inhabitants. And yet within days the police would be tearing the place apart in their search for clues. Later they would come to believe that Holly and Jessica were murdered in the dining room of this brick building, and their corpses driven away from the scene using this vehicle to be burnt in a ditch. For all its ordinary appearance, this was a house of horrors.

On Thursday, 8 August 2002 the first hint that it might be significant came to the attention of the assembled media. They were told that the man who occupied the tied property owned by the college, caretaker Ian Huntley, was among those who had seen the missing girls during the course of their final walkabout the previous Sunday evening. The police had already questioned Huntley and taken note of the fact that he had spotted Holly and Jessica strolling through the grounds past his front door that night.

He was one of a handful of people who may have been the last to see the girls alive. Naturally enough, the media were eager to speak to Huntley, if only to capture the drama of such a potentially crucial sighting. Several had spoken to him before in passing, or to ask him for directions around the college or permission to use the electric sockets to power laptops and camera chargers. Now it seemed he might be able to offer some handy quotes as well.

I called at 5 College Close that afternoon in the hope of speaking to Huntley about his sighting of the two girls. He was not in, but Maxine Carr answered the door. At the time nobody had any inkling of the crucial part his girlfriend had played in the story of the murders, and I was expecting only to carry out a routine interview consisting of a few words, the kind of job journalists do every day. However, when she opened the door Carr made an immediate and striking impression. Not in the sense that she seemed stunningly beautiful or even attractive, but in her anxious demeanour. In Soham at that time it was commonplace to see people looking under strain; the whole town was in shock over the girls' abduction. But Carr appeared flustered and exceptionally worried for Holly and Jessica's safety.

She told me Huntley, whom she referred to as her 'partner', was not in, and I asked her if she would spare me a few words herself, to help with the police appeal. I wondered if I and my colleague, photographer Helen Atkinson, could come in to talk through what she could say to help jog people's memories and bring the girls home. Amazingly, given the facts of the case, she agreed with only a moment's slight hesitation. It was clear from the serious set of her face that she considered this duty to be very important, and that's why she would carry it out, despite the inconvenience.

Standing to one side and holding the door open, she invited us in across the threshold, where I wiped my feet on a coconut welcome mat, and allowed us to turn left and walk in front of her into the living room. She was, I thought, very polite. In fact, I was to learn later that her politeness concealed a far more sinister motive. For the room immediately behind the front door, through another internal doorway, had been stripped completely, from top to bottom, of every piece of furniture and cleaned of every speck of dust. This was the room where Huntley is thought to have murdered the two girls on the night of Sunday, 4 August, and he had scrubbed it frantically to get rid of every tiny drop of blood, flake of skin or thread of hair. Carr, her jaw locked in an expression of concern, was in reality concerned about something other than the girls' safety. What she was scared of was getting caught. So she blocked our way into the killing room with her body.

Turning away from the scene of the crime, we passed through a passageway just a few feet long and lined with wood painted in white gloss. I noticed the planks in the panelling shone as though they had just been polished. We went into the living room and again the impression of cleanliness was striking. The glass ornaments on the mantelpiece gleamed against the pastel-coloured wallpaper; the television in the far right-hand corner, near the rear window, had no dust stuck to its screen. Light shining into the room from both sides, through windows at the front and the back, bounced off all the surfaces. Underfoot, the flower-patterned carpet was so well vacuumed I felt apologetic about walking on it, and the curtains, also with a floral pattern, appeared to have just been washed. It couldn't have been more immaculate if it had been a show home for a new housing development. Especially for a travelling reporter who was in the middle of a month-long stay away from home in various hotels, the spotless room had a certain domesticated appeal. But again this image was a terrible lie. The room was so clean not because of Carr's homely pride but because the couple had been desperate to scrub away all traces of the children Huntley had killed.

Carr must have been terrified to have two members of the most inquisitive body of people on earth prying around in this place. That's probably the reason why much of her conversation consisted of grumbling about the press. 'I've never had anything to do with journalists before,' she said. 'I didn't really think about what they were like, but I've met so many of them in the last few days and, I'm sorry, but they're just prats. They're really pushy, nasty people, they won't leave us alone. They keep asking to speak to me and to Ian and, you know, we want to help but what can we do?' She waved a business card given to her by a reporter. 'This bloke was round at the door earlier and I swear there's something wrong with him. He kept asking all these daft questions, I couldn't tell what he was on about. I don't suppose you're all like that – you seem all right.' The hostility towards the media, who were providing an important – it was later to emerge, crucial – role in solving this crime, might have seemed odd. We might have thought it suspicious if it were not for the fact that the same hostility is shared by such a large proportion of the general public in Britain.

Carr had offered me a seat on her sofa, facing the mantelpiece, and I was patting Sadie, a friendly animal with a very glossy coat, on the head. Huntley's girlfriend was speaking in a soft, quiet voice with a strong Lincolnshire accent. I commented on her being from somewhere in the north, and we shared a few words about our respective northern origins. I asked her if she liked it down south, and she said things had been good since they'd moved, and that Soham was a nice place. 'You can tell that from the way people are about this,' she said. 'Everyone wants to help, they were all here for the search. Ian went with them.'

Her hair was shoulder length and the dark-brown, wavy strands were slightly tangled, giving her a harassed appearance. She was wearing a dark-blue blouse with flowers of a lighter colour printed on it. It looked like it was made of some synthetic fabric and was neither expensive nor fashionable. She also wore a pair of simple black trousers and around her neck a plain silver chain adorned with a jewelled crucifix. On her finger was an engagement ring.

I asked her about Huntley's sighting of the girls, speculating that it could be highly important. She said: 'It's terrible – I only wish we had asked them where they were going. Ian talked to them for a couple of minutes as they came walking past the front of the house. If only we knew then what we know now, then we could have stopped them or done something about it. I was in the bath and he was out washing the dog in the garden. They asked him how I was doing because I used to teach in their class last term and they knew I was applying for a job. He said they were really happy and fine. They went off afterwards over the bridge towards the library.' As Carr gestured towards the back of her house with a vague sweep of her right arm, I noticed her skin was extremely pale, as if she rarely went outside, even at this warm time of the year. The only trace of make-up I could see was red lipstick, which stood out against the pasty white of her complexion. Her cheeks were slightly puffed up and spotty, suggesting she was not in the peak of health. Her eyes were small and a very dark brown. They had a shielded, almost deadened look about them. She didn't smile once during our encounter.

Then I asked about Holly and Jessica. What sort of children were they? Carr had been the teaching assistant in their class for five months before the end of the school year, and it was obvious she must have known them well. Other teachers at the school had already told me that she had a particularly close rapport with the two friends. In the words of one: 'Of all the teaching staff, she was probably the one they could relate to best. She was the youngest and the nearest to them in age and interests. They didn't see her as some kind of person above them, she was closer to being a friend. There's no doubt at all that she was the favourite for both of them. They'd stay behind and talk to her after class. They talked about all sorts of things, not just school work. I think they liked to confide in her because she never told them off and she was more like an older sister figure than a teacher for them.'

From what Carr told me, she appeared to return the girls' affection. She spoke of them warmly, saying: 'They're lovely, really bubbly girls, kind towards everybody. They used to come in and hold my arm and talk to me. They were very friendly.' She confirmed what the other teacher had noticed about how Holly and Jessica would treat her as a grown up-sibling, and added: 'They would say things like, "You're so cool, Miss Carr." I think they felt they could talk to me because I am a bit younger than the other teachers. They thought I was more on their level – like a big sister.'

Astonishingly for someone in her situation, Carr showed no sign of any difficulty chatting about the girls, and her conversation went far beyond what was necessary for a short newspaper interview to help with the police appeal. She described the girls' very different characters, explaining how Jessica was the more assertive of the two. 'Holly is more feminine, a bright girl, very good at English,' she said. 'Jessica is more of a tomboy – she loves playing football and swimming. They are both very nice, quiet girls, but Jessica is the sporty one – you don't see her very much in a skirt. I make a joke with her sometimes about that, and she said to me once that when I get married she wants to be my bridesmaid. She said she would even wear a dress.'

Speaking with her arms folded across her chest, Carr also said that the girls were still very childlike at heart, despite being at the age when they were growing up. 'Holly and Jessica like doing all the usual things other girls their age do. They're very close friends and they play together all the time. They're both very good at school and they like using the computer. They know how to send emails and use the internet.'

Carr had very clear ideas about some aspects of the girls' disappearance. Unlike the many people of Soham who said they were completely baffled and in the dark as to what might have happened, she had some certainties. 'They are both bright kids,' she said. 'They wouldn't get into a car with someone they didn't know. They would have kicked up a right stink if somebody tried to get hold of them, they would have screamed out. They're not the type to run away, they're both very well behaved and good. They're not naughty at all, they're happy girls who aren't any trouble. I don't think they'd do anything silly – they're both quite sensible.'

At the end of the school year in July, Carr had been forced to tell the pupils who adored her that she would not be coming back after the summer holiday. It was an emotional moment, and Carr told me how it had moved Holly to break down in tears. Without a trace of guilt in her eyes, she said: 'Holly was very upset. She started crying when I told her I didn't get the job. On the last day of school, Holly gave me a card with a smiley face on the front and a poem inside. She gave me a box of Roses chocolates as well.' Carr seemed proud of Holly's affection for her. I suggested her card would make a good photograph to put in the paper to jog people's memories and also, perhaps, to move an abductor to compassion. She agreed immediately, and went off to get it, leaving Helen and I for a few seconds alone in a room which nine days later would be the subject of an unusually intensive forensic search. It appeared that Carr had stored the card in the room where the girls were killed.

Even at the time and without the added significance it would later attract, this thank-you card was difficult to look at without experiencing a sickness in the stomach. In the middle of its front cover was a big, round, smiling face drawn in a childlike hand. The picture was the image of innocence, an innocence which had since been cruelly shattered. Across the top the girls had written: 'I'll miss you a lot' and had dotted the page with thank yous. At the bottom was a reminder of their familiarity with mobile phones and text messages: the abbreviated 'C Ya around school'. Inside the folded white cardboard the girls had written a poem:

> It's class 12's special TA
> We will miss her a lot
> And we will say
> See you in future Miss Carr,
> Don't leave us, don't go far.

The card was signed 'C Ya' and 'Miss Ya luv Holly', with several kisses along the bottom. Carr explained that Holly had given it to her along with a big hug. She held the card out to be photographed and then posed for a series of pictures holding it in her hand. She spoke about how 'nice' it was with a look in her eyes which was neither sad nor angry but blank. She looked numb, emotionless, and I interpreted that expression as one of shock. Perhaps I was right.

After Helen had taken several shots of Carr and the card from all angles, we decided it was time to leave the teaching assistant in peace. I apologised for taking up so much of her day and she said it had been no trouble, adding: 'I just hope they find them.' I left thinking I'd met a pleasant, sympathetic young woman whose flaws were nothing more serious than a lack of beauty and a slightly dull manner. In fact, she'd been sharp enough to hoodwink me and other journalists and policemen who talked to her during the hunt for the girls. The next time I saw Carr she was in the dock charged with helping the killer escape justice. As Huntley himself might have put it, it beggared belief.

13

OPERATION
FINCHAM

O n Monday, 5 August dawn broke over a town in
turmoil, its people certain a terrible crime had been
committed. Although Sunday night had been cold and wet,
the girls had left home in clothing no heavier than their
Manchester United shirts and summer trousers. Their
disappearance had clearly not been planned, and the
prospect of spending all those hours shivering in the dark
did not seem a likely schoolgirl prank. Knowing the
children and families as they did, the local population felt
Holly and Jessica's disappearance could not have been
intentional. They now began to volunteer by the hundred
to help in the search. USAF personnel from the Lakenheath
and Mildenhall airbases joined in, ready to search the
thousands of acres of fen, fields, forests, rivers and ditches.

While Huntley and Carr carried on their caring couple

act, the police were setting a huge operation in motion. A police computer selected at random the code name 'Operation Fincham', and with the investigation declared active thousands of calls began to pour in. Holmes 2, the police computer system used for major cases, was installed to deal with them. The Cambridgeshire force's investigation team was soon built up to 250 officers. Children disappeared from Soham streets as a cloud of fear spread over everyone – parents, grandparents, relatives, friends. The town became a mental and physical prison, with children locked away and adults acting as scared warders, wary of strangers and suspicious of one another.

The task of finding human remains is a huge problem for the police. It might be thought that a rural town like Soham, with 8,700 inhabitants, and where most people know everybody, would not be difficult to search, particularly as it lies in a flat landscape. But a flat terrain gathers water, and in the surrounding fens, the ditches alone total hundreds of miles in length. A searcher could be feet away from a child's body in the muddy channels and not see it. Missing just a few yards of ditch, stream or river can mean that the whole area must be searched again. Police diving teams were called in but covering this huge area of watery land was slow work. The extensive local grassland presented its problems too, especially with the abundant summer growth, as long grass, tussocks, nettle beds, hedgerows and rough ground are all able to conceal a slight body or its parts.

Squads of searchers went out under police direction, using sticks to poke into every hideaway over many square

miles of territory, in what was becoming the largest
manhunt ever mounted in Britain. Their belief that the
girls may have been alive somewhere drove them on. Some
worked at this very demanding task for 16 hours a day
almost non-stop. Any moment a movement of the hand or
stick could reveal a sight so gruesome no one would know
how to face it. But at least then they would know. That
thought kept the hundreds of searchers going.

Of course, it was still sometimes possible to think that
the girls would be found alive and well but, as the areas
covered grew larger, time rushed by and weariness kicked
in, it became harder to see anything but a tragic end. As
one searcher realised: 'This really makes you see what the
police have to put up with. I'm frightened of finding
something because it would scare me to death, but I've got
to keep trying for the families. After a day of this I'll go
home to my own kids and get scared even if they go into
another room.'

In some respects the hours of searching were the most
hopeful for the families, but their statements reveal the
turmoil beneath the strong exteriors. The Chapmans tried
to believe that their daughter's screams would have been
heard if she had been abducted because 'she has a loud
voice'. The thought conveys their nightmare. To support
them Detective Superintendent David Hankins said: 'We
hope this is an adventure that has gone wrong. But we are
told that they took no money and no food. I would have
thought that they're getting cold, wet, hungry and dirty.
Police inquiries to track missing children are of the highest
priority because of their vulnerability. You can be assured

that we will work tirelessly until they are found.' Mr Hankins, father of a 10-year-old daughter, added: 'This affects us all. Our thoughts are with the parents and friends, and we are thinking of the anguish that they are going through.'

That anguish drove the lonely figure in the red bobble hat and wellingtons, with the expression on his face which somehow stopped any other searcher from asking what he was thinking. Kevin Wells was in among the thick of the search around Soham for 16 hours on the first day alone. Police with mobile phones and radios marshalled the search around him.

As the search grew the police called in yet more reinforcements, and by the end of the operation 700 officers had taken part. A helicopter with thermal-imaging equipment and an RAF Tornado overflew the ground without finding anything. A bloodhound brought from Wales also turned up nothing. In Soham the police were joined by hundreds of journalists from newspapers and TV stations all over the world. Every hotel in the town and for miles around was full, and the streets were lined with satellite outside-broadcast vans.

The visitors found a frightened place which had changed overnight for its residents and which was now changing them all for life. 'This is the sort of place where I've always told my daughter to run to the nearest house if there's any problem. Now what do I tell her?' said Terry Skelton, whose 12-year-old daughter, Samantha, knew the missing girls. 'We watch the television news and sometimes we cry. I don't want to go out. Nobody is going out,' she said. Most parents were forced to agree. 'It's terrible for them, staying indoors in the school holidays,' said Tracy Grinstead, keeping a close eye on her children as she visited the supermarket. 'But it's a terrible thing that has happened, and I don't want to let them play alone.' The Reverend Tim Alban Jones noticed how few children were now out on the streets, and commented: 'We are all anxious for our children these days, but people are saying to me that they are so shocked that this had happened in their own backyard.'

Usual police procedure allows a period of several days to go by before parents are asked to make a public appeal for missing children to return. In this case, however, the rule was dropped and at 3.30pm on Monday, 5 August the parents made the first of their tearful appeals for the return of Holly and Jessica. Faced with the enormity of the girls' disappearance, the families spoke with an urgent simplicity and sincerity. Leslie Chapman said: 'We forgive them, just come home. Jessica knows how to use the phone. It's a mystery she hasn't phoned us.'

The next day the police arranged for England football captain and original wearer of the girls' number-seven shirts, David Beckham, to add his voice to the appeal for the pair to return. In a statement broadcast on TV he said: 'Please go home, you're not in any trouble. Your parents love you dearly and just want you back.'

In these attempts the police and families were buoyed up by experience of other cases in which children had gone missing, only to turn up safe and well. Two fathers whose daughters were kidnapped for three days by paedophile

Alan Hopkinson on their way to school sent messages of hope and support. They told the Soham parents to 'have faith' and believe Holly and Jessica would return just as their girls had. But, even though people tried not to think about it, other, more tragic cases stuck in everyone's mind. Sarah Payne was abducted from a field in July 2000 and, though the eight-year-old's murderer was captured and convicted, she did not survive. More recently, Milly Dowler was another girl who had paid the price of running into a murderous man in the wrong place.

By the morning of Wednesday, 7 August the police investigation had encompassed the physical search of Soham and the surrounding area, 2,500 phone calls, 400 door-to-door interviews and the stopping of 700 cars. Nothing had been found. Two detectives who helped to catch Sarah Payne's killer, Roy Whiting, joined the inquiry. The ingenious Detective Inspector Chuck Burton arrived from the Derbyshire force with the Catchem computer system, designed to build offender profiles. More than 60 specialist search team officers were drafted in, including some who had worked on the Milly Dowler investigation in Surrey and the investigation into the murder of 16-year-old Danielle Jones in Essex. Other personnel, from Scotland Yard, the Hertfordshire and Northamptonshire police forces, the British Transport Police and the RAF, also added their expertise.

In an attempt to jog memories the investigators staged a reconstruction of Holly and Jessica's final walk. On Saturday, 10 August two young actresses retraced the girls' route around Soham dressed in the bright-red Manchester

United number-seven shirts. They had been given haircuts matching those of the missing pair, and the actress playing Jessica wore the same jewellery. At least 200 local people watched with mixed emotions as the reconstruction began. The Reverend Alan Ashton, the local Methodist minister, had to urge calm because expectation was enormous: 'We're living in reality. This is not a detective story, there's no Inspector Morse to make everything all right.'

A week into the inquiry and the Cambridgeshire Constabulary were feeling the heat. Though officers were doing everything they could to track down the missing girls, some sections of the media began to criticise their lack of progress. The force's Chief Constable, Tom Lloyd, came in for a public slating for being on holiday in France while the inquiry was under way. Mr Lloyd had to bow to pressure and return to work. Journalists discovered the police station in Soham had been closed down 11 years earlier and a CCTV network planned for the town had yet to be put up.

But most damaging of all was the series of false leads which emerged to exasperate the police, the families and the public alike. Trails which produce nothing are normal in any investigation, but during the Soham case each tip was mercilessly scrutinised by the press. The police were criticised for reacting too slowly, or for running up blind alleys. The first false report was from Tina-Marie Easey, who claimed she had seen the girls on the A10 near Little Thetford. Her sighting caused momentary relief, but it turned out to be wrong. The police issued a plea to youngsters not to wear Manchester United shirts as it was feared the children's parents could not take any more false hope.

Other red-herring leads came thick and fast. Taxi driver Ian Webster reported seeing a man driving a green Vauxhall Vectra or Peugeot with two children inside on the evening of Sunday, 4 August. The man swerved as he 'thrashed out' out at them. The report, which caused a sensation when Webster complained of police slowness, created an avalanche of work. There are 103 green Vectras and 71 similar Peugeots in Cambridgeshire alone. Throughout Britain, the numbers are 2,500 Vectras and 8,992 Peugeots. Each one had to be traced. But Webster's car clock was an hour fast. When he saw the car, Holly and Jessica were still roaming the streets of Soham. A white van 'cruising' the streets was also eliminated, along with dozens of other pieces of information.

After feverish speculation that the girls had been 'groomed' by an internet paedophile, the police announced that the pair had not visited chatrooms or sent emails during their last session online.

Rumour in the town spread with astonishing rapidity, and often achieved the status of fact before the police had the chance to dispel it. One such story was that a sex offenders' hostel had been secretly opened nearby. Another said Terence Pocock, sentenced to life imprisonment in 1985 for the rape and stabbing of two 13-year-old girls in the Soham area, had been released. Neither rumour was true. Things got worse when the *Sun* and the *Daily Express* offered huge rewards for information leading to the recovery of the girls. In what many criticised as a cheap publicity stunt, a total of more than £1.25 million was now on offer to anyone who could bring Holly and Jessica home.

The police were walking a tightrope. They needed to keep the media spotlight focused as it was their best hope of turning up a lead. But the media could also be their biggest enemy in throwing up false trails. With such trails emerging and being eliminated one by one, attention focused on local sex offenders. The information on sex offenders held by Cambridgeshire's police and social services included 266 registered individuals and 433 others known to be resident in the county. Five profilers drew up a picture of a suspect. The hunt concentrated on a local man, probably with previous sex offences, aged between 25 and 40. Without a crime scene the profilers worked on probable scenarios. Most offender profiles fitted their conclusions. This formed the basis of the next police strategy: a direct appeal to the abductor through the media.

This unusual approach was the idea of Detective Superintendent David Beck. For several days he would now try making this kind of appeal to the abductor of Holly and Jessica. Carefully chosen pictures of Jessica were released, aiming to humanise her in the mind of the girls' captor. They showed her looking relaxed and happy on a family holiday only the week before she was snatched. 'Don't let these photographs become some of the last pictures that the family have to remember Jessica by,' DS Beck said.

As we have seen, the Wellses and the Chapmans also

bravely agreed to help with this strategy of making a direct appeal to the abductor. Their moving displays of torment and grief were intended to work on the kidnapper's mind and play on any vestiges of human feeling he might possess. In the hope that the girls were indeed still alive somewhere, the police tried to tempt the abductor to switch on Jessica's mobile phone and leave an electronic trace of his location. On Wednesday, 14 August DS Beck appealed to the kidnapper on television, asking him to get in touch by midnight and saying instructions had been left in a message to Jessica's mobile phone. According to the theory, the abductor's weak spot was that the kidnapping had become far more serious a situation than he had intended, and he would want to read the detective's message because he was looking for a way out. Unfortunately, Holly and Jessica were, in fact, long dead, and their abductor had no human feelings which could be described as weaknesses, other than a terror of being found out. DS Beck's midnight deadline came and went, and the manhunt remained frustratingly fruitless.

Already by Tuesday, 13 August the Wellses and the Chapmans had had their hopes raised many times, only to have them dashed – but worse was yet to come. A week earlier a jogger from Newmarket had contacted his local police to report noises and some mounds of disturbed earth he had noticed on the night the girls had disappeared. His statement was logged along with many others, but, with the focus of the hunt now shifted to Newmarket following the evidence of the taxi driver Ian Webster, the police went over it again.

Between 10.40 and 11.10 on the Sunday evening, while running through the woods at Warren Hill, the jogger heard what he thought were horrendous screams, possibly coming from young girls. He also saw some mounds of freshly disturbed earth in the area on a hill above Newmarket race course. Rumours spread that 'graves' had been found, and police family liaison officers were instructed to brace the families for shattering news.

The jogger returned to the disturbed earth with a police officer at 4.25pm on the 13th. At 5pm Henry Cecil, the world-famous horse trainer, heard a helicopter fly over his garden near Newmarket. He too heard the news which millions were dreading. By nightfall tents stood over the mounds as 100 police officers conducted a fingertip search in preparation for digging, overseen by forensic experts. The experts were concentrating on two areas at Warren Hill, some 30 yards apart and 200 yards from the road. As arc lights were switched on among the trees the scene took on a gruesome atmosphere. The grim, horribly slow and careful work began as the whole of Britain watched the evening news. Soham was tense, and as a mark of respect all three pubs on the High Street closed soon after the police began to dig – not even world war had made that happen. Around the streets people met in groups of two or three, making painful conversations about the dig. No one was used to talks like these.

Everyone had the girls and their waiting families in mind. For them this was going to be agony. Family liaison officer Detective Sergeant Chris Mead knew what effect his unannounced visit would have when he called at the Wellses' home that evening at 5pm. 'They knew from the look on my face what I was about to tell them was not good news,' he said. The task of telling Kevin and Nicola was difficult enough, but, as he described the mounds to prepare them for the worst, Holly's brother, Oliver, came in to listen. He kept standing by the phone, waiting. His distressed father felt: 'He's coping with it in his own way. I don't feel he fully understands the full seriousness of the situation – he's only 12 years of age – but he's missing his sister.'

The Chapmans were also told what was happening, and they waited behind closed doors for what followed. The Wells family could not bear the intrusion of radios or television, so all sets were switched off. They drank tea, but no one could watch the video someone had put on. No one could sleep. Holly's grandmother, Agnes Wells, felt: 'It was one of the longest nights of my life.' At 4am the first mound had been dug, with nothing found except a badger sett. The families felt hope and despair as they waited for news of the second. At 6.30am this too turned out to be a sett. The screams the public-spirited jogger had heard were probably badgers.

The two families went back to hoping and dreading, hugging and weeping. Kevin Wells said: 'It's been a roller-coaster of a night. We found out the news officially at about 6.30am. It's been extremely upsetting. We were fearing the worst but we are still here to carry on the fight and while there is still a glimmer of hope we shall carry that fight on.' Leslie Chapman also showed the courage of the two families in his statement about their night of terror: 'In the early hours of the morning came the immense relief with the news that it was not them. But the questions start again: where are they? It has been a very tense and traumatic night.'

The false lead of the badger setts left Soham and people across the world on a knife edge of hope and depression. The tension had been racheted up by several notches. A watch was being kept on ports and airports, the 'green car' lead was still being followed up and cars throughout Britain were being traced, but conventional policing using information obtained directly from the public had so far provided only a series of false trails which had swallowed up resources and precious time. The benefit of following these to their conclusion was that the ground was cleared for what could be the true lead which might bring the children back. But time was running out, and everyone knew it.

The Wellses and the Chapmans had now endured 10 days of torture, while millions who had witnessed their ordeal on TV or in the newspapers suffered with them. The nation willed on the police to somehow, anyhow, bring all this to an end, and restore the lives of these brave people. The frustration had reached fever pitch.

14

THE
BREAKTHROUGH

By Friday, 16 August it seemed detectives might never crack the mystery of what had happened to Holly and Jessica. But, behind the scenes, one line of enquiry was beginning to look promising.

Officers had identified Huntley early on as a possible suspect in the case, and they had been watching him carefully, ever since he had come forward more than a week earlier as one of the last people to have seen the girls. The surveillance had included a thorough study of every word he and Carr had uttered. Psychologists had even been drafted in to study their body language in the hope that some clue might emerge. Detectives questioned Huntley informally on many occasions, arriving at his home for what they presented as a friendly chat. They took him through his movements on the evening the girls disappeared, going over his statement again and again in the hope that he would slip up. The quiz became so exhaustive that Huntley complained to his father, Kevin: 'What do they expect me to do, make something up?'

The police held back from arresting the pair partly because all they had on Huntley was a suspicion. A criminal record check under his name did not reveal any previous offences as his file had been wiped clean after the charge of rape in 1998 had been dropped. Another reason why the couple were not arrested at this stage was that detectives still hoped the girls were alive somewhere. If Huntley and Carr had been holding Holly and Jessica captive, then at some point they might have led the police to where the girls were imprisoned.

However, as the days passed, the team who had Huntley and Carr under observation felt increasingly sure that they had the right suspects in their sights. By Thursday, 15 August telephone engineers working on the trace left by Jessica's mobile phone had managed to narrow its location on 4 August down to a much more precise area. Peter Bristowe, an expert in telephone technology, studied reception patterns in the area of the girls' final walk. He found that most of their route was covered by a mast at Soham Football Club, but there were some 'hotspots' in the town in which mobiles connected to the network through a mast at Burwell, about five miles to the south. He established that the final signal given off by Jessica's pay-as-you-go phone was emitted at 6.46pm on Sunday August 4. This 'goodbye signal' had been received, not by the mast at the football club, but by the mast at Burwell. The only

Burwell mast hotspot on the girls' route that evening was a small area which included Huntley's house and the immediate vicinity. So it was almost certain that the handset had been switched off and disconnected from the network at, or very near, 5 College Close. Armed with this information, the police redoubled their surveillance of Huntley. As one officer put it, they were now watching him 'like a hawk', using every available method.

Police colleagues in Grimsby were also back on the case, trawling through their files in more detail to find any record of the names Huntley, Nixon, Carr, Capp or Benson. They discovered that, in 1998, Huntley had not only been accused of rape but had been charged with the offence and had been on remand in jail when the case against him was abandoned. Following Carr's TV and newspaper appearances from Thursday, 8 August onwards, calls had started to come in from Grimsby pointing out that, far from being in the bath at her home, Carr had actually been in that town on the evening the girls disappeared. Several witnesses said she had been walking around Grimsby with her mother during the period she claimed she had been in Soham.

Now believing they were looking at a serial sex offender who had constructed an alibi, detectives needed something concrete to tie Huntley to the disappearance of the girls. In effect, they needed him to make a mistake. His situation at the heart of the murder hunt in some ways helped their efforts against him. Surrounded by police officers hunting him and journalists desperate to find out every last detail about the case, he was in a precarious position. The police decided to let this state of affairs continue for a period, hoping the pressure would make Huntley crack. Here was one of the key features of the Soham investigation: the police's use of the press as a powerful tool in their armoury. However, one of the problems with Huntley being embedded in the investigation was that he never had the opportunity to make a false move. He knew if he blinked he would be caught, and he displayed an astonishing ability to survive in these circumstances.

The string of false leads during the final days of the hunt was in some ways helpful to the Huntley investigation. For one effect of these was to offer the suspect periods of security when police and journalists were no longer breathing down his neck. The hope was that he would relax and betray himself by saying or doing something incriminating. Another effect was to leave the area clear for the police to search unhindered by crowds of inquisitive journalists. That is not to say that the police deliberately manufactured false leads, but a conscious effort was made to get the media out of the way.

On Thursday, 15 August a press conference was held 35 miles from Soham Village College, at police headquarters in Huntingdon. The explanation given at the time for this choice of venue was that Detective Superintendent David Beck was unable to spare the time to come to Soham, and he came under criticism from journalists for never having been to the town in his life. Like much of the criticism of the police during this period, it was made without knowing the full facts. Detectives wanted the college grounds empty so that Huntley could be free to make a move. For much of the next day the college was closed to the press altogether.

Meanwhile, officers decided to crank up direct pressure on him in the belief that this would force him into a false step. Their daily questioning sessions became more pointed and less friendly. Although still using a soft approach, they were letting the caretaker know he was a suspect. Huntley, cunning as ever, did not fail to read the signals. He told Carr: 'I know they're going to arrest me.'

It was also on Thursday the 15th that the police deployed another tactic to pile the pressure on Huntley. A community conference was to take place that evening in the assembly hall of Soham Village College, with the ostensible purpose of allowing the people of the town to voice their concerns to the police about the progress of the investigation. Its real purpose was to leave Huntley rattled. The man who was by now the prime suspect spent the late afternoon trying to cram as many chairs as possible into the hall in preparation for the event. He exchanged mumbled greetings with a few of his neighbours and shook his head when some mentioned how distressing it must be for him to have been one of the last to see Holly and Jessica alive. He pinched the bridge of his nose to stem the tears and held his arms out wide in a gesture of desolate frustration. 'I can't believe it,' he kept repeating, then carried on with his work.

Townspeople straggled into the assembly hall in twos and threes, slowly swelling the crowd until more than 400 people were gathered. The evening was close and thundery, and with the large crowd squashed into the hall the atmosphere was humid and uncomfortable. Sealed off from the media waiting outside, the people of Soham were told that the clue to the mystery of the missing girls lay within their own community. 'Is there someone around you, friends or neighbours, who are doing anything differently?' asked Detective Inspector Simon Causer. Maurice Audley, a one-time commando and former chief superintendent of the area, strode forward. He faced the audience and thundered: 'I want you to go home and talk to your wives, husbands and children, to cast your minds back to that Sunday. Talk to each other and think about the neighbour on your right-hand side, the neighbour on your left-hand side. Are they a Darby and Joan couple you have known for years, or a family you can vouch for? Look at all your neighbours in your mind and ask yourselves: "Can I vouch for them, am I quite certain they have nothing to do with this abduction?"'

The appeal was met with prolonged applause. And in the hot, sweaty hall the people of Soham were looking to their left and to their right. Fully in view was the murderer Huntley, leaning against the wall to the left of the stage. A photograph of the event shows him standing next to a local churchman, listening intently. His features betray nothing more than an expression of concern, but the message had hit home.

With Huntley and Carr so firmly in the frame and with hopes dashed that Holly and Jessica were still alive and being held against their will, the police decided to act. The first hint that the inquiry was about to take a dramatic turn was dropped by Leslie Chapman at the press conference on the morning of Friday, 16 August. Holding on to his wife's hand, Mr Chapman said there was 'a lot going on behind the scenes that the police aren't telling the media about'. His remark went almost unnoticed as the two sets of exhausted parents left the press conference.

Following yet another heart-rending appeal, there appeared to be little happening that Friday afternoon. With the story from the press conference already written up, most of the journalists milling about in the college car park were busy sorting out their hotel rooms for the weekend at the Rutland Arms in Newmarket, or calling their families to explain why they wouldn't be coming home for the twelfth day in a row. Few noticed two plainclothes officers turn up in separate vehicles at the caretaker's house at the far edge of the car park, and no one realised that what happened next was the most significant point in the case.

At 3.45pm the detectives knocked on Huntley's door; finally, they had come to get him. It was the moment Huntley had been dreading throughout 12 long days and nights, but still he did not lose his composure. They asked him if he would come to the police station to answer some questions and he agreed without a murmur of dissent. Asked if she would come too, Carr likewise agreed immediately. Huntley, wearing his blue polo shirt, walked quietly out of the house, got into the waiting unmarked police car and was driven away. Seconds later, Carr did the same.

The move was witnessed by my *Daily Mirror* colleague Lorraine Fisher, who, like everyone else, did not realise the importance of what had taken place until afterwards.

She later described the scene: 'There were no police in uniform, squad cars, sirens or flashing blue lights. Instead, when Ian Huntley and Maxine Carr were driven away, there was nothing but an air of calm. I walked past the school caretaker's house shortly after detectives had driven up in two unmarked cars. Huntley stood by his little red car talking to a taller man who I took to be a detective. But this was nothing unusual. Over the past fortnight I'd seen police saying hello to the caretaker and chatting away in his company. So as he stood talking, albeit looking a little sheepish, to the officer, the sight did not strike me as being suspicious.

'The door was wide open and shadows of people inside could be seen as Maxine walked around. There was no air of menace, desperation or rush. To the layman it looked like a plainclothes policeman had dropped round to check a fact or get a piece of information. But just minutes later Huntley and Carr were being gently escorted out to the unmarked cars outside. There was no struggle, no raised voices. In a car park full of people it had passed off almost unnoticed. But within 10 minutes journalists were told to get to the college for an urgent announcement. It was only then that the penny dropped. As I'd watched police had made that vital breakthrough.'

The moment when the police caught up with Huntley and Carr was recorded by an astute photographer from the local press agency, Masons. In what have become famous pictures, Huntley is seen looking anxiously at the plainclothes detective, his brow furrowed deeply. Carr, wearing a tight-fitting Italian World Cup shirt, looks pale and shattered. She has obviously resorted to make-up to hide her fragile state, her lips being freshly painted bright red.

The scene was the start of a turbulent night for the pair. Huntley was taken to Ely police station, five miles away, for questioning, while Carr was deliberately placed much further afield, in Peterborough police station, where she would be free from Huntley's influence. Detectives asked both of them to make another statement; they were trying to break down Huntley's alibi. They wanted Carr to admit she had been in Grimsby on the evening of 4 August – but both suspects stuck to their story. At 9.30pm the pair were released and allowed to meet in room 384 of Holiday Inn at Histon, Cambridgeshire, a location which was kept secret from the media. The police hoped they would relax a little and say something incriminating during the encounter; they had bugged the room and monitored every word they spoke. Huntley was then driven to his father's home in Littleport and Carr was left at the hotel. A police guard was placed on both locations, and again both were bugged.

Kevin Huntley's house was a modern brick bungalow with a flat roof and a caravan in its overgrown garden. It was tied to the job he had as caretaker of a school in the town, and he had lived there with Lynda since the couple got back together at Easter 2002. Huntley arrived there under police escort at around 3am. He found his parents in a state of shock over their son being linked to the horror in Soham. Earlier that night they had spoken out in a desperate attempt to defend Huntley and persuade the world he was innocent. Unfortunately, much of what they said had indicated the opposite, not least because they confirmed what journalists had discovered earlier in the day: that Huntley had previously been charged with rape.

Lynda, a cleaner at Soham Village College and a dinner lady at the school where her husband worked, was in tears and highly agitated. Kevin, who had managed to suppress his own feelings of horror, struggled to calm her down. Lynda said: 'Ian and Maxine are the sweetest couple. He is the gentlest person. This will ruin his life – he nearly had a nervous breakdown last time he was arrested.' According to his mother, Huntley had been tormented by the girls' disappearance, even seeing them in his sleep. She added: 'He kept saying: "I close my eyes at night and all I can see is me speaking to them."'

Kevin and Lynda did their best to back their boy, but their words revealed that even they were not sure he was innocent. Kevin said: 'I'm 99.9 per cent sure he didn't have anything to do with it. No one can be totally sure.' Few parents could have entertained even the slightest possibility that their son had committed such a horrific act. The couple were being comforted that night by their younger son, Wayne, who within days would make up his mind that his brother was 100 per cent guilty.

Meanwhile the police continued to probe every nook and cranny of Huntley's home, the college and its grounds. Remembering the caretaker said he did not have the keys to the hangar, they examined his key ring and discovered he had lied. They subjected the hangar to a painstaking search. In the early hours of the morning of Saturday, 17 August, PC Tim Wade found the fragments of the David Beckham shirts and trainers, which Huntley had hidden in

216

a bin. He noticed what looked like a mound of rags lying in the bottom of the third bin along from the door. PC Wade recalled, 'I bent over and picked up something that felt like clothing. I pulled it out and saw it was the remains of a red T-shirt. I could see black and white lettering on the shirt – it was obvious it was the word "Beckham" and the number seven. I could smell a strong smell of smoke- it was obvious it had been scorched.'

The shirts, along with the trainers and other clothes, had been hidden beneath a black bin bag. Huntley's fingerprints would later be found on the plastic. It was the vital piece of evidence detectives had been looking for. Following the discovery, the police acted swiftly. They swooped on Huntley and Carr once more in two separate operations. Huntley was seized at his parents' home at 4.20am and Carr in her Holiday Inn hotel room five minutes later. This time both suspects were placed under arrest.

My *Daily Mirror* colleague Lorraine Fisher was still hard at work, sitting outside Kevin Huntley's bungalow in Littleport. Earlier he had told her that his son wanted to give an interview about the day's dramatic events. She had been invited into the house to speak to Huntley, but feared for her safety in the presence of the killer and was waiting for back-up in the shape of a photographer. Lorraine was chatting to Wayne Huntley through the window of her car when the police arrived. She described the scene as follows: 'Suddenly, out of nowhere, a silver car screeched in front of mine. Two men in fleeces and jeans leapt out and shouted at Wayne: "Who the hell are you?" They were detectives, and, as he told them, I realised we were surrounded by unmarked police cars. Unknowingly we were in the middle of a dawn raid on the Huntleys' home. An officer demanded to know who I was. "Press," I said immediately. "Well, drive to the end of the road and wait there," he ordered. They then stormed the house and arrested the man they suspected of murdering Holly and Jessica.'

When officers arrived to seize Huntley, he appeared to be in a terrible state. He was dribbling constantly and foaming at the mouth, mumbling gibberish. The appearance of going insane was another act he had made use of on a number of occasions. According to friends of his ex-wife Claire, he had performed this routine several times during their brief marriage and once on his stag night. This time he was to use the dribbling act to get himself locked up in Rampton.

The discovery of the fragments of the shirts and trainers in a room to which few besides Huntley had access made officers certain they had found their man. The fact that these remnants were badly burnt also led them to believe that Holly and Jessica were dead.

Later that morning, when Detective Chief Inspector Andy Hebb announced the arrests of Huntley and Carr, the wording of his statement reflected these conclusions: 'In the early hours of this morning police search teams recovered from Soham Village College items of major interest to our inquiry. These items have been preserved at the scene and will be subject to a comprehensive forensic examination, a process likely to take some considerable amount of time. In the last few hours a 28-year-old man and a 25-year-old woman have been arrested. The 28-year-old man has been arrested for the murder and abduction of Holly Wells and Jessica Chapman. The 25-year-old woman has been arrested for the murder of both girls.'

DCI Hebb's belief that the girls were dead was soon proved accurate. Hours later their bodies were discovered lying in a ditch near RAF Lakenheath and the hamlet of Wangford, in the neighbouring county of Suffolk. While Huntley and Carr still sat in their police cells, the police had cordoned off a huge area of countryside around the spot where Keith Pryer had found the bodies. Forensic experts would carry out a painstaking search of the girls' last resting place, but the corpses were so badly destroyed in Huntley's pyre that pathologists struggled even to identify them formally. The bodies lay in the ditch being examined for more than two days, and scientists working on them carried out an unenviable task; the sight of what remained of the two girls would have made anyone sick.

Finally, at around 8.30pm on Monday, 19 August, the bodies were moved from the ditch, carefully placed in bags and put into a private ambulance to be taken to Addenbrooke's Hospital, in Cambridge, for further examination. A small huddle of police and reporters waited at the site near the northern edge of the airbase to witness the scene. Out of the dense mist rising from the fens, the ambulance crawled at a speed of less than 20mph, the middle vehicle in a convoy of three. Leading the way, a marked police car flashed its headlights repeatedly through the mist; the lights shone out brightly in the gathering dusk. Nobody in the little crowd said a word. The only sound was the tyres of the ambulance scrunching over some loose pebbles on the single-track lane as it passed. It was the end of the mystery of the girls' disappearance, an end no one wanted but everyone had come to expect.

Having found the suspects and the bodies, it was only a matter of time before the police would start the legal process against Huntley and Carr. However, officers were aware that the bodies had yielded little forensic evidence, and only some fragments of burnt clothing and a collection of circumstances linked the couple to the crime. They wanted more, in particular to crack Huntley's alibi and turn Carr so she would give evidence against him. They applied for and were granted two extensions to continue to question the couple without charge until Wednesday, 21 August.

After the couple's arrests, police interrogators were to make little progress with Huntley, but they did manage to demolish some of Carr's lies. Detective Constable David York got her finally to admit that she had been in Grimsby when Holly and Jessica went missing. Speaking hours after her arrest, she said: 'I wasn't in Soham on August 4. I wasn't in Soham on August 3. I wasn't in Soham on the Monday either. I came back to Soham on Tuesday. I was actually in Grimsby and the reason I told police I was at home was because my partner, Ian, was accused in 1998 of attacking a girl, raping a girl. It went to court. He was put in a prison and a bail hostel or whatever. He had a nervous breakdown and everything else. When I found out he was the last person to see them at that time, to speak to them, I didn't know what to do.' Carr admitted something DC York already could prove. By now, many who saw Carr in

Grimsby had contacted police. Caught out in a lie, she wanted the police to believe she gave Huntley an alibi not because he had murdered two girls, but because of a rape accusation from four years ago. The tactic bore the hallmark of Huntley's conniving inflluence, and Carr let slip, 'Ian told me to tell you that.' She didn't explain why she was certain Huntley had been the last to see the girls.

During the interview Carr appeared surprisingly relaxed. She said she didn't need a solicitor. Half way through, she asked for a break so she could eat a strawberry yoghurt. DC York guided the conversation towards Carr's relationship with Huntley. He wanted to know how they met, how they felt about each other. He pressed her lightly, encouraging her to talk as much as possible. Carr described how she had been introduced to Huntley at Hollywood nightclub in Grimsby, how the couple had moved in together less than a month later. Was it love at first sight? 'Dunno. For me, maybe,' she replied. Huntley, she admitted, had been violent towards her on one occasion.

She said, 'He got quite angry with me and I was just shouting at him and bantering at him. I can't really remember what the argument was about, but he just slapped me across the face. Because of my bone structure in my face it bruised, but it wasn't like a fist in my face or anything. It was just like a sort of slap sort of thing, to shut me up really.'

DC York picked over Carr's story, gently pointing out the weaknesses in her account. She had come back from Grimsby earlier than planned, she had been spotted scrubbing tiles in her house so hard the paint came off. But

Carr insisted this was all in keeping with her being an exceptionally caring, dutiful girlfriend. She said, 'Someone's got to look after Ian and feed him up if he's going to be out on the streets searching with you guys all night – he can't cook and clean for himself.'

The house, she said, had been in a terrible state when she returned from her trip away. 'Ian don't bother to wash up,' she said. 'He leaves his pots on the side of the draining board, there's crumbs on the side. He just slouches about on the couch, he's not bothered. The cushions aren't where they should be, just been slobbing about, just having his glasses where he has a drink, crisp packets and sweet bags. His goodie chocolate packets down where he's been watching telly and his ashtray ...'

Carr was apparently still certain that her man had done nothing wrong. His arrest was a big mistake; she knew he was innocent. She said: 'If Ian had killed somebody, do you really think he'd be walking around doing his job, being happy, because that's not the kind of person he is. He's a very emotional person, and he would have fallen apart if anything like that had happened. I know Ian better than you or anyone in here, even probably better than his mum. I wouldn't lie about a murder. I wouldn't lie about two kids that I know. Yeah, I might love him, but I wouldn't do those kind of things. I had three and a half years with Ian. They were good. Nothing made me think: "Oh God, I have got to get away from this man". I love him.' Carr claimed Huntley called her at 6.30pm on the night of the girls' disappearance. She said he told her Holly and Jessica had passed by and had asked after her before leaving unharmed.

In fact, telephone records would show the couple had spoken at 6.24pm, before the girls had arrived at 5 College Close. For all her protestations, Carr was lying yet again.

On Tuesday August 20 Detective Constables Kim Bowen and John Taylor made one last attempt to break down her story. The conversation was recorded as follows:

> DC Bowen: What I will tell you is, that Ian has been charged, formally charged now with two murders.
>
> Carr: Uhhhhhh!
>
> DC Bowen: The murders of Holly Wells and Jessica Chapman.
>
> Carr: He can't have!
>
> DC Bowen: And I'll tell you what else: forensically, his fingerprints have been found on the bag that the clothing was in.
>
> Carr: No!
>
> DC Bowen: At the hangar.
>
> Carr: No!
>
> DC Bowen: Now you wanted facts, and you wanted to know about the forensic side.
>
> Carr: (*crying*) No, he can't have been, it can't have been, he can't have been.
>
> DC Taylor: He's killed Holly.
>
> Carr: No he hasn't.
>
> DC Taylor: He's killed Jess.
>
> Carr: (*crying*) No!
>
> DC Taylor: Open your eyes Maxine, look at the facts.

Carr: It's not Ian, he could not have done something like this and then carry on as normal.

DC Taylor: He couldn't unless you helped him.

Carr: I didn't bloody help him.

DC Taylor: Who was the last person to speak to Holly and Jessica?

Carr: Ian, I think.

DC Taylor: Whose fingerprints are on the bag?

Carr: Ian's.

DC Taylor: Who lived near Wangford?

Carr: Ian.

DC Taylor: Who goes to Lakenheath spotting aeroplanes?

Carr: He hasn't been up there for ages.

DC Taylor: Who had a false alibi?

Carr: Ian.

DC Taylor: Who had his house cleaned by Maxine?

Carr: He didn't have his house cleaned by Maxine ... it's my flaming house ... I ain't got nothing to do with this at all, and he ain't got owt either.

In the event, despite being told she could face a long jail term, Carr would not turn her back on Huntley. And he would barely say a word, looking blankly at detectives as if he didn't understand their questions and repeating his pretence of going mad. On Tuesday, 20 August officers decided to call time on the performance. Huntley was sectioned under the 1983 Mental Health Act and transferred from police custody at 2am into the hands of doctors. He was taken off to Rampton, to be detained indefinitely and have his state of mind examined.

That afternoon, two detectives from the Cambridgeshire force drove to see Huntley in the high-security hospital, where they charged him with the murders of Holly and Jessica. This move, announced by DCI Hebb at the force's headquarters in Huntingdon, was followed at around 11pm by the laying against Carr of a charge of attempting to pervert the course of justice. In spite of Huntley's playing at insanity and Carr's acting the innocent, officers were determined that both would stand trial, he for murder and she for shielding him from punishment.

15

A WORLD
IN GRIEF

The news that Holly and Jessica were dead and that their bodies had been found came as a sickening revelation to their parents, the community of Soham and millions of others across Britain and the world who had been following the story of their disappearance. Although many had felt from the beginning that the search for the girls could only end like this, the realisation of those fears after 13 days of clinging on to every glimmer of hope still came as a heartbreaking shock.

Within hours of Keith Pryer making his grisly find, bouquets of flowers began piling up in the yard of St Andrew's Church in Soham and next to the police cordon sealing off Huntley's house. Messages of condolence had begun flooding in by letter, email and fax from all over the world, and an enormous outpouring of public grief was under way which would rival the scenes of mourning that followed the death of Princess Diana in 1997 or the death of the Queen Mother earlier in 2002.

Above all, the discovery of the girls' bodies was, in the words of Kevin Wells, a 'hammer blow' to the parents. Kevin, Nicola, Leslie and Sharon were struck down by a tragedy most could not bear even to imagine. With remarkable bravery and dignity, Kevin was to speak to his friend James Fuller, a journalist for the local newspaper, the *Cambridge Evening News*, of how the parents' nightmares became reality.

'When the bodies were found it was a terrible time,' he said. 'Even though we had known in our heart of hearts that they might not be coming back, the discovery still came as an absolute hammer blow. Also, at that time, dealing with the emotions of Oliver [Holly's brother], Nicola, grandparents and extended family members was very traumatic. Having everyone round here and telling them Holly was definitely dead was tremendously harrowing and obviously something you never think, as a father, you will have to face. Once we had got to that stage we had to wait for DNA samples to confirm that the bodies were Holly and Jessica but the police told us they were as sure as they could be it was them. From then there was a definite shift in emotions. This crime had been committed against my daughter and her friend and the initial disbelief of it all turned to a great deal of anger. This was coupled with feelings of frustration and helplessness for Holly and really just finding it all so hard to comprehend. They were dark, dark days.'

The news that everyone had dreaded was broken in a police press conference on the afternoon of Sunday, 18 August. Acting Deputy Chief Constable Keith Hoddy made the following announcement to the assembled media: 'It is with great sadness that I have to tell you the following news. It may be some days yet before we are able to positively identify the two bodies. However, we are as certain as we possibly can be that they are those of Holly and Jessica. Holly and Jessica's families have been told this terrible news. Before I say anything else I suggest we pause for a moment in silence in memory of these two little girls and out of respect for their families and their many hundreds of friends.'

The 150 members of the press then stood in silence with Mr Hoddy and his two colleagues, DCI Andy Hebb and Cambridgeshire Constabulary spokesman Matt Tapp. Even in this gathering of hardened reporters and policemen, the faces were pale and drained and many were close to tears. The scene would be repeated that afternoon at early-season football matches and other events across the land as thousands marked the passing of Holly and Jessica with silent tributes.

Mr Hoddy read statements from each of the families. Sharon and Leslie Chapman said: 'We would like to thank everyone for their kindness and support during this very tense and traumatic time, especially friends, family and family liaison officers. While we appreciate your support and all your assistance in this very trying time, we would like you to respect our privacy and allow us some time alone.'

With the same quiet dignity Nicola and Kevin Wells said: 'Although still numb after losing our gorgeous daughter Holly, please accept our heart-felt thanks for everyone's help and support throughout this traumatic fortnight.' The emotional announcements were made in the car park next to St Andrew's churchyard, which would soon be submerged in a huge sea of flowers. The bouquets would be piled several feet high, submerging the gravestones and stretching the length of the grass area outside the ancient parish church. The scene was a graphic testimony to the fact that what had happened in Soham had become a national and international sorrow experienced by millions who could share the feelings of the parents. It was a sight so moving that Holly's grandmother, Agnes Wells, collapsed as she looked at the bank of flowers which expressed the deeply felt sympathy of so many strangers.

The extraordinary power of that universal sympathy was also seen earlier that day in the joint Church of England and Methodist service held in St Andrew's Church. Normally the Reverend Tim Alban Jones could expect 50 people to attend for Holy Communion at 9.30am. On this occasion 500 filled the place to overflowing, and those who couldn't get in stood outside in the churchyard. A single bell pealed as the mourners grieved with quiet dignity. Many wept with their dark thoughts, while others' faces showed they were too shocked to weep any more. The solemn air of sadness and grief overcame everyone who shared this experience, welding them together. As one young mother said: 'I am not a regular churchgoer. But I just wanted to come here to be among people, to feel part of the community at this terrible time.'

During his sermon the Reverend Alban Jones, a father of three children under eight, described the town's sense of shock: 'Only one week ago, we could not have thought that we would be sitting here this morning facing the worst-case scenario. In spite of all our hopes and prayers, this is what we have all been fearing and we are now staring in the face the outcome which we were most dreading. Our community of Soham has been in a state of shock since we first heard of the disappearance of Holly and Jessica and the sense of shock has, if anything, deepened as time has gone by. The distressing and disturbing developments that we heard about on the news yesterday mean that we are even more stunned and, if possible, sent even deeper into shock. There are scarcely words available to sum up our sense of disbelief that all this has happened in Soham. This past fortnight has rocked our whole community ... The whole town feels in some way violated by the disappearance of Jessica and Holly.'

Outside the church, speaking to the press, the vicar added, 'There is, I would say, evil at work when two delightful, charming 10-year-old girls are abducted and not seen for a fortnight. Now we are faced with the prospect that their bodies have been found. There is no other word that can be used to describe that.'

The hymns chosen for the service brought a lump to many throats as the congregation sang 'The King of Love My Shepherd Is' with its heartbreaking line 'In death's dark veil I fear no ill'. The aptness of the texts, chosen weeks before, felt uncanny – Matthew 15, verses 10–20: 'For out of the heart came evil intentions, murder, adultery, fornication, theft, false witness, slander. These are what defile a person.' In what seemed like an omen, the service was interrupted by a deafening clap of thunder.

As the congregation left, their emotions were stirred once more by the growing carpet of flowers and messages laid out in tribute to the girls. Already the flowers stretched almost the full length of the churchyard. By the following day, when Holly's parents felt strong enough to pay a visit, the floral display had become startling in size. More than 10,000 bouquets had been delivered. All day every day the messages and flowers would continue to pour in, along with hundreds of teddy bears and toys.

That Monday Kevin and Nicola Wells spent 45 minutes taking in the extraordinary scene. They walked the length of the churchyard, in the High Street, examining the messages of sympathy which had been left for their daughter. About every 10 paces they were stopped by someone who felt compelled to offer their condolences. Nicola finally burst into tears and had to be led away by her husband, who wore a Manchester United shirt similar to the one his daughter had worn on her final walk. A resident of the town said: 'You have to admire their courage. The fact that they can come out and thank everyone like this shows you what kind of people they are. The whole of Soham has been out laying flowers down and everybody is in tears.'

The rows of toys and flowers were nine deep by mid-afternoon. Among them, lying in the soaking grass, was a single pink rose with a lone word: 'Why?' A pink posy of carnations from a mother and grandmother carried their fervent wish: 'Jessica and Holly. May they play together in heaven just as they did on earth.' A Manchester United shirt carried the note: 'In our hearts we hoped you were safe, but someone took you away. The theatre of dreams awaits you.' A message on the church gates read: 'I wish I could have been there in your hour of need.' A note pinned to a bunch of home-grown yellow chrysanthemums said: 'Soham's heart is broken.'

While the residents tried to express their innermost powerful feelings, their grief was being shared all over the world. At 8am that morning St Andrew's Church was telephoned by a woman in Australia who wanted to know the correct address to send flowers. Others came themselves to join in this outpouring. Ipswich taxi driver Steven Baldry, 33, travelled for three hours and said: 'I wondered whether to come. It's a small town and maybe they want to be left alone. But, now I've seen this, I know I've done the right thing. There are flowers from all over. This is unbelievable.' The Interflora van driver, while unloading a van full of bouquets, explained to the vicar that he would be back soon with three more full loads. The cards with the flowers showed they had been ordered in Manchester, Belfast, London, Edinburgh, Cardiff, Birmingham and many other places.

Five-year-old Brittanny Gibbs from Derby came to lay flowers with a card which read: 'Two angels in heaven. Now let's stand united against such evil for future generations. Our thoughts are with you.' A Manchester

United scarf stretched between two roses with a photo of the club's star, David Beckham – the girls' idol – carried the question on everyone's mind: 'Why? Holly and Jessica, you touched us all.'

Inside the church a thousand candles made the large stone altar too hot to touch as they flickered for the two girls. A helper sent out for some more returned saying that the shopkeeper had refused to accept any money. The Reverend Alban Jones felt: 'This has touched hearts up and down the country, friend and stranger alike. It is quite extraordinary. There is not a parent here who has walked away with a dry eye.'

Alison Smith, visiting the church with her two young daughters, her mother June Woods, 74, and the girls' friend, Hattie Fletcher, six, said: 'They have sat in front of the telly and listened to the news and haven't uttered a word. They wanted to come here and light a candle to send a message of support. How do you explain something like this to a six-year-old?' The sympathy which gripped so many at this time had rarely been seen before. The scale of the public's interest could be seen in the viewing figures for television news programmes. On 19 August BBC news pulled in 11.5 million viewers. Another 4.5 million people watched ITV news on the same evening, while Channel 4 also doubled its news audience to 2.1 million. Even the late-afternoon bulletins drew 3 million viewers each.

Many messages from the flowers and gifts were recorded in a book of condolences, along with emails from around the world. Within 20 hours of its opening more than 22,000 people had emailed the Cambridgeshire Constabulary's website dedicated to mourning Holly and Jessica. Another 9,000 emails were received on the first day at the website set up by the county council, and many thousands contacted the Soham community website.

By 21 August messages were coming in at the rate of one every two seconds, from Australia, Israel, Zimbabwe, Bahrain, Brazil and Dubai. A Sri Lankan man said: 'I was following your daughters' case from day one on Sky News, here in Sri Lanka. Each day I hoped would bring better news than the previous. The final outcome has been incomprehensible and intolerable, even for me, someone from a war-hardened country thousands of miles away.' From France, Margaret and Chris hoped the new technology's ability to bring instant support would be a comfort: 'Words can't express how we feel, but I hope that the love which will come to you through this modern medium may help in some way.' The web of human sympathy stretched even to war-torn Israel, where a 13-year-old was thinking: 'I heard the dreadful news of the two girls, Holly Wells and Jessica Chapman. I've been following the latest news every day, hoping it would turn out well.'

Parents in particular found it frighteningly possible to identify with the families. 'As a mother of a child of the same age, I am at a loss as to what to say: I have worried with you; I have hoped with you; I have despaired with you; I have cried with you,' wrote a woman from Somerset.

The size of the public's reaction to the Soham tragedy meant that no building in the small town could accommodate the crowds who wanted to mourn Holly and

Jessica. Only an ancient cathedral could provide the space, the dignity and the atmosphere of deep spirituality needed.

Above the fens, the massive Norman bulk of Ely Cathedral seems to float like a ship on the flat green waters. The troubled people of this land, as they have done for centuries, took their burden into its mighty body for some kind of resolution on 30 August, at a service of celebration and remembrance for Holly and Jessica. The girls were buried in small, separate and private funerals on the following Monday and Tuesday, but this service was intended as a public expression of mourning.

The roads were closed at 8am. Five hundred invitations were available for police personnel who had been involved in the case. The remaining seats were taken by family members and by the residents of Soham, who had queued every morning in the previous week to get a ticket. The girls' classmates from St Andrew's Primary School attended, along with their teachers, as did the six family liaison officers, who had provided a 24-hour service for the Wells and Chapman families.

In all, the twelfth-century building contained more than 2,000 individuals who wanted to take part in the occasion. To signify that their attendance was part of the healing process, the celebration of two lives, the congregation had been told to avoid a sombre mood and dark funereal colours. Jackets of fuchsia, lilac, purple and turquoise among the rest in the massive nave and transepts lent another layer of meaning to the event. Nicola Wells and Sharon Chapman both wore lilac tops.

The families were escorted from the Bishop's House by

the Bishop of Ely, the Right Reverend Anthony Russell, and the Reverend Alban Jones to the south entrance just before the service began at 5pm. They were welcomed by Canon John Inge, vice-dean, who led them to their seats at the top of the nave. Their friends, family and neighbours were behind them, along with the eight senior policemen who had organised Operation Fincham. These included Detective Chief Inspector Andy Hebb, Detective Superintendent David Beck and the man who was now leading the investigation, Detective Chief Superintendent Chris Stevenson.

The coloured afternoon light, streaming through the jewels of the stained glass mellowed by centuries, played on the strained faces as the congregation fought their tears, or just wept as quietly as they could. People sobbed and gazed at the floor as hot tears rolled down their cheeks. The courage of the families, their quiet dignity and pride in their lost children overwhelmed the assembly. Their loss appeared in its true light – so cruel and unnecessary, uncalled for and undeserved, brought about by one man at random, but so immense and lasting for ever. The grand nave and its transepts were lined with sobbing figures.

The Reverend Alban Jones spoke of the need for the community to move on from its paralysing grief on behalf of the 'bright and cheerful' 10-year-olds. He said: 'Would not the best and most lasting memorial to these two lovely girls be a change for the better in how we behave towards each other? Holly and Jessica were two trusting and loving girls, and the way they lived is surely the right pattern for all of us. The very worst thing that could happen as a result of what took place in Soham is that a whole generation of children should grow up without being able to trust anyone. Today's service is a small milestone in our shared journey of grief and sorrow. It is our hope that we might perhaps draw a line under one phase of our grieving and begin to look forward.' Then the hymn 'All Things Bright and Beautiful' rang through the huge chamber.

Though these thoughts could not begin to explain the tragedy, give an account of why such a dreadful thing had happened or put the world back to where it was before Huntley invited two 10-year-olds into his front room, they expressed the need of the people of Soham to survive and live their lives beyond it. Howard Gilbert, Head of Soham Village College, also captured the mood of the town in a nutshell when he said: 'I long to hear our children laugh again.'

The climax of the occasion came when Kevin Wells, in his red tie and dark suit, took to the altar to read his poem in memory of Holly. 'The Soham Rose' expressed his grief so simply and directly that it shattered the composure of all. In a voice controlled by superhuman effort, Kevin read:

> *Your right to grow, to mature and play,*
> *So cruelly denied in a sinister way.*
> *Attentive and caring, a parent's delight,*
> *But so young at heart, needing comfort*
> *at night.*
> *The garden so quiet, the house is too,*
> *But pausing for a moment, we can still*
> *sense you.*

Your trusting nature and desire to please all,
Allow us your family to remain walking tall.
Our memories, now shared, with the
Nation's hearts,
Small crumbs of comfort, now it is time
to part.
We will never forget you, heaven's gain
as it knows,
Is simply you Holly, our beautiful
Soham rose.

His words would later be echoed in the naming of a rose created in memory of Holly and Jessica. The delicate, orange-petalled bloom, unveiled at the 2003 Chelsea Flower Show, was a moving symbol of the girls' innocence and beauty.

16

THE MOB

With Huntley and Carr arrested and charged, the huge public outpouring of grief over the deaths of Holly and Jessica would soon turn to anger at those held responsible for the crime.

This process was perhaps inevitable given the horror of what had happened to two innocents, but the sense of outrage was perhaps inflamed by the fact that the accused were not stereotypical middle-aged, flasher mac-wearing paedophiles. Huntley and his girlfriend had been in positions of trust; parents everywhere had to depend on caretakers and teaching assistants. Their betrayal of trust was a crime millions felt angry about, and the fact that one of the suspects was female made matters even worse. Such was the fury towards the two suspects that people across the country were ready to see them lynched. The police had to keep secret the locations where they were being held, for fear of vigilantes taking revenge, and wherever they went security was tight.

In the event, the public expressed its anger towards the Soham couple at the earliest possible opportunity. When Carr appeared in court before magistrates in Peterborough, her precise location had to be published for the first time after her arrest. She had been held at the police station just 75 yards from the courtroom for the best part of the previous four days, but that fact had not been made public at the request of the police. Her court appearance, however, had to be put on the record by law. Unlike Huntley, she had not managed to avoid the event by pretending to be mad. So, while he was tucked away in Rampton, she had to face the public, and face them alone.

As expected, on the morning of Wednesday, 21 August a crowd gathered outside Peterborough Magistrates' Court, a red-brick building in the town centre. Slowly, as Carr's scheduled appearance time of 9.30am drew closer, the numbers swelled. There were young people and old, children, mothers, office workers on a coffee break, tramps. Across the street people opened windows in the shops and flats and were leaning out. It seemed everyone in this medium-sized town on the edge of the fens knew Carr was about to arrive.

During the next hour came scenes which left no doubt just how furious people felt towards the Soham suspects. Peterborough, considered to be so typical of staid, unflappable middle England it even had a *Daily Telegraph* column named after it, was about to witness the actions of a hate mob. At 9.28am class 12's former teaching assistant was led from the cells at Bridge Street police station. She emerged from the back door with a blanket over her head, shielding herself from the sight of photographers who had scaled the building's wall using stepladders. She was bundled into the back of a police van and driven the short distance to the court protected by around 70 officers who lined each side of the route. As the vehicle came into view round the corner of Bridge Street, the crowd issued a thunderous yell. People screamed abuse while the van drove slowly up the street and disappeared into the basement car park of the building.

The sounds of hatred must have been a shock to Carr, for she arrived in court looking ghostly pale and haggard. Flanked by three women security officers, she was ushered into the courtroom to face the magistrates and dozens of reporters. Amid a silence broken only by the rustle of notebooks being opened, she managed a brief, nervous, sickly smile at one of the court officials before her eyes fell. From then on she seemed desperate to avoid the gaze of any of those who stared at her. First she studied the wrought-iron crest behind the magistrates' bench. Then she stared at the blank television screen hanging from the ceiling opposite her.

Wearing a black, short-sleeved T-shirt and blue denim jeans, she seemed bewildered as she blinked and played with her unkempt hair. Those in the crowd of journalists who had met her before she was accused noticed a marked deterioration in her appearance. Her weight seemed to have plummeted, her cheeks were hollow and her greasy skin had developed an unhealthy pallor. She wore no make-up or jewellery; gone were the engagement ring and the crucifix that previously hung around her neck. The silver chain had been removed by the police in case she used it to strangle herself.

The atmosphere in Court One was one of tangible tension as all eyes remained fixed on the 25-year-old in the glass-fronted dock. Then the clerk formally read out the charge, '... that between August 9, 2002, and August 18 in the County of Cambridgeshire with intent to pervert the course of public justice you did commit a series of acts which had the tendency to pervert the course of public justice, in that you gave false information to police officers in a criminal investigation and that is contrary to common law.' Principal Crown Prosecutor Marion Bastin then set out the details of the case as Carr listened, her features blank. Carr's expression changed dramatically as it was revealed that the charge carried a maximum sentence of life imprisonment. Suddenly it all seemed to be too much for her and she slumped forward with her head bowed to the floor. She remained in the same position for several minutes, her hands clasped at the back of her neck, pulling at her hair as if she was trying to block everything out.

Carr did not speak during the proceedings except to give her name as required by the court. Even then her voice was barely audible, a quiet, high-pitched mumble that everyone strained to hear. When the court clerk read out her address in Soham she simply nodded to confirm it was correct. Just a couple of yards away the man who had become the public face of the Soham investigation, Detective Chief Inspector Andy Hebb, watched her every move. But if she was aware of his gaze she did not show it. Her own solicitor, Roy James, addressed the court only briefly and did not make any application for bail. The magistrates rose for a brief adjournment and on their return the chairwomen of the bench, Gill Wild, told Carr she would be sent to Peterborough Crown Court for a preliminary hearing and would be remanded in custody until then.

The teaching assistant was then led from the courtroom to face the crowd outside once again. She had been in the court building for nearly two hours, and those waiting for a glimpse of her had grown impatient and restless. The talk had been of the horror of Holly and Jessica's deaths, and the hatred had been stoked by reflections on the angelic appearance of the girls and Huntley's sick burning of their bodies. Roy James later tried to dampen the public anger against his client by pointing out that she had not been charged with murdering the girls. But, in the eyes of many, Carr's attempt to help Huntley get away with murder was almost as reprehensible as the act of killing itself. And few who followed the case could come near to forgiving her for the days of torture her actions had inflicted on the girls' families.

Everyone on the street outside the court that day had followed the case, and no one was in a forgiving mood. At 11.25am the simmering silence of the waiting hundreds suddenly exploded into fury as Carr's police van came into view. Sirens blared and a police helicopter hovered overheard while the steel shutter which sealed off the underground car park slowly wound up to reveal her white marked van with its blue lights flashing.

The screams of the 500-strong crowd rose to a terrifying climax as Carr was driven up the concrete ramp beneath the building. People surged forward and a few managed to burst through the police lines. The pavements were packed five deep with people of all ages – pensioners, young mothers, teenagers, even young children. Some waved banners and jeered, others stood silently holding up pictures of Holly and Jessica. And some of the younger children were in tears, shocked by the hatred they saw. Everyone seemed to be yelling. Even workers in nearby shops stepped outside to add their voice to the ear-splitting sound.

Mother-of-one Rhonda Bailey, 28, pelted the van with eggs as it accelerated away from the court. Another two women broke through the police cordon, one managing to slam her fists into the side of the van. A woman in her twenties had to be held down by officers after she kicked out at the vehicle as it swept by, led by a police Volvo estate and followed by a marked four-wheel-drive Mercedes.

The roads had been sealed off to clear a path through the traffic and make the departure as fast as possible. Around 20 minutes before the dramatic exit, the police had drafted in reinforcements to control the crowd. A group of 20 officers jogged out of the court and pushed the crowd away from the ramp leading out of the underground car park. They joined the 70 others who had already formed a ring round the 75-yard run leading back towards the police station. One policeman picked up a brick and removed it from the scene. Amid the uproar, his caution was understandable. The people were screaming: 'Murdering bitch', 'Rot in hell' and 'Scum' at the van, which disappeared down Bridge Street and off towards Holloway Prison, in north London, where Carr would be locked up awaiting trial. Five minutes after her exit the crowd spotted DCI Hebb leaving the court. They greeted him with a spontaneous burst of applause.

If there had been any doubt about the way the public felt towards Huntley and Carr, it was now thoroughly dispelled. Now and probably for the rest of their days, the Soham suspects were hated like no other criminals since Ian Brady and Myra Hindley. Among the many placards on display in Peterborough that morning was one which read: 'Bring Back Hanging'. From the behaviour of this crowd, it seemed the people of England wanted Huntley and Carr dead.

17

SUICIDE WATCH

While Carr was facing the wrath of the mob, Huntley had managed to hide himself away in Rampton for 50 days of observation. Doctors at the hospital, near Retford, Nottinghamshire, would watch him constantly. He was put under what is known as level three observation, which means he was watched by a minimum of three nurses at any time, who made notes every 15 minutes about his actions and behaviour. Huntley's every move was recorded in exhaustively detailed reports which were studied by leading experts in mental illnesses like schizophrenia, paranoia and depression.

As Huntley played the laboratory guinea pig, he made the best of a standard of living far superior to that afforded the average inmate in prison. According to sources at Rampton, Huntley appeared relatively happy during his time there and said he had 'no complaints'. Nurses tried to ensure that his life and those of other patients were as near normal as possible. Like everyone else, Huntley was given access to cash in his own bank account to spend in a hospital shop, and was allowed to order items from Argos and Woolworths catalogues. Money he had saved from his job as a caretaker was paid into his Rampton account, and he also received £13 a week in pocket money from the state, a sum to which every patient was entitled. He had the option of earning extra money by carrying out menial jobs around the hospital, but refused to work.

Staff at Rampton described Huntley as a 'model patient' who never caused any trouble during his time there. The child killer was put on the hospital's Derwent Ward. His room, unlike the average prison cell, was tastefully furnished with an en suite bathroom, television and CD player. He had the use of £50,000 worth of gym equipment and the Manchester United fan liked to play five-a-side football with fellow patients. He was seen less often in the 25-metre swimming pool or the large library.

Huntley would spend his money at the hospital's Good Buys shop, where patients – including fellow child killer the former nurse Beverly Allitt – socialised at the weekends. Each week he ordered sweets, crisps and fizzy drinks and every month bought *FHM* magazine. Rampton is proud of its high culinary standards and serves meals on a three-week rotating menu. However, Huntley, always partial to chips and chocolate, hated the hospital diet of rich, well-cooked food and refused to eat. During his time there his weight dropped from 12 stone to less than 10.

He benefited during this period from supportive visits from his mother Lynda and brother Wayne. On one occasion Lynda gave him a £20 phone card. Wayne brought him a food parcel of bananas, some chocolate bars and a bottle of orange squash. At times Lynda gently held her son's hand as if to reassure him as they talked. When their time was up she slowly got to her feet and embraced him, wiping away tears. Huntley asked if she could bring a Chinese takeaway the next time she visited.

As in his life before his arrest, Huntley was something of a loner at Rampton. He spent most of his time in voluntary isolation in his own room, shuffling about barefoot in a blue smock with Velcro tabs. But he did make one friend, in the shape of 40-year-old serial rapist Seymour Howell, who had been jailed for life in December 1984 at the age of 22, for raping two women weeks after being released from a mental hospital. The two men would talk during meal breaks, exercising in the gym and playing pool.

Huntley's existence at Rampton is recorded in a letter he sent to a penfriend: 'The staff (most of them) are kind and take good care of me. We play chess, scrabble, table tennis etc. I am watched 24/7 by two people [nurses] even on the toilet. Most embarrassing. The meals are terrible. The papers say I have put on weight. But, in fact, I have lost nearly two stone. Soon I will vanish. Thank you for writing to me once again. It amazes me how many people I don't even know take the time to write to me. I seem to have a bit of a fan club which I find very strange under the circumstances. I have received letters from afar as

Germany. It helps a lot to know there are people out there that are supporting me though.'

As well as support from correspondents across Europe, Huntley could call on the services of a large team dedicated to his care. These included a registrar, occupational health therapist, language and speech therapists as well as two psychiatrists and two psychologists. However, he seemed acutely aware that some of these people would soon see through his feigned madness.

On 8 October 2002 doctors decided it was time to bring Huntley's charade to an end. In a report put before Peterborough Crown Court, they dismissed his mental illness as a sham and said there was no reason why he should not be treated like any other suspect. The document, written by Rampton's Dr Christopher Clark, concluded: 'Ian Huntley is not suffering from any form of major mental illness – in particular he is not suffering from schizophrenia, paranoid disorder, manic depressive psychosis or a significant mood disorder such as depression. His long- and short-term memory and concentration are entirely normal, apart from a mild degree of difficulty in concentration when he's feeling anxious – which is quite normal. Ian Huntley doesn't currently suffer from any form of mental disorder making it appropriate for him to receive treatment in hospital. It's felt appropriate he be remanded in a normal form of custody.'

The findings clearly came as a blow to Huntley. He began to shake and rub his leg uncontrollably, wringing his hands, muttering to himself, gulping and licking his lips. He knew he would now face trial for murder and that, despite all his efforts, he would at last be going to a normal jail.

Later that day the killer of Holly and Jessica arrived at Woodhill Prison, in Buckinghamshire. As he was led through the building to his cell, the man now known as Prisoner JG5778 faced a barrage of abuse. Inmates crowded to the doors of their cells and screamed at him, shouting 'Nonce' and threatening to kill him. It was with relief that he reached his specially constructed cell in the segregation unit. The choice of Woodhill as Huntley's new home reflected the high degree of concern at the Home Office about his case. The prison was considered to be the flagship of Britain's top-security Category A institutions. Among Huntley's fellow inmates was Britain's most dangerous prisoner, Charles Bronson, veteran of 27 years in jail and perpetrator of a string of violent attacks and hostage-taking in prisons across the land. Another Woodhill inmate was killer and kidnapper Michael Sams.

But, of all the prisoners at Woodhill, Huntley was the most notorious. Builders had spent weeks making him a cell isolated from other inmates and with vantage points from which he could be watched by warders and surveillance cameras 24 hours a day. Six specialist officers were assigned to him at all times. His clothes and slippers were made of paper so there was nothing he could use as a noose to hang himself. Even the furniture in his cell was constructed so it could not be broken or taken apart to be used as a tool or a weapon to harm himself. His bed was a concrete plinth with a sheet of foam rubber as a mattress. His table and chair were bolted to the concrete floor. The lavatory pan, wash basin and even the wall mirror were made of polished steel instead of glass or ceramic so they could not be smashed and the shards used to cut veins or arteries.

Warders described Huntley's tailor-made cell as a 'prison within a prison'. Walls were knocked through, connecting his cell with the two neighbouring ones. That gave him a 'soft cell' living space 25 feet square and made guarding him easier. He was allowed a rowing machine and an exercise bike. He was also allowed treats such as Mars bars and Kit Kats. Among Huntley's possessions was a small radio cassette player. A fruit bowl, usually with apples and bananas, was on display. He kept a box full of letters and paperwork on a table. Above his bed Huntley had attached five photographs to the wall, glued with toothpaste. One was of Carr. On the window opposite, arranged so as to hide the bars, he had stuck some messages sent by well-wishers, including cards depicting angels, flowers and scenes of heaven. One of these was from his fiancée; it was signed 'Love from Max'.

Officers believed Huntley's cell was so secure that it was physically impossible for the killer to harm himself. But at 3am on 9 June 2003 their confidence in Huntley's security was shattered when they found him slumped in a coma on the floor of his cell. He had swallowed 29 tablets of the antidepressant Amitriptyline and without treatment would be dead within hours. In some ways Huntley's attempt on his life was entirely predictable; in letters from jail he had discussed suicide, writing: 'Suicide has crossed my mind in the past. I have had some feedback regarding my requests to go on a normal location and or some form of association. The answers to both were no, as they fear for my safety. Some officers are concerned about the suicide potential if I have no supervision from staff as I have now.' These thoughts had already been reflected in Huntley's actions, for three weeks earlier he had tried to hang himself.

However, this time Huntley came very close to achieving the release of death. Staff were mystified as to how he managed to do this while under surveillance 24 hours a day. It later emerged that he had plotted the attempt with characteristic cunning. Doctors had prescribed him Amitriptyline to combat his bouts of depression, and Huntley knew full well that the drug can induce drowsiness even in small doses, and in larger doses effectively shuts down the body. Instead of swallowing his daily prescription, he hid the pills under his tongue, spitting them out into his hands when the warder's back was turned.

Huntley's cell was searched frequently and stripped down at least twice a week, but during these occasions he managed to hide his stash of tablets by wrapping them in teabags and storing them in his rectum. Every few days he loaded some pills into a clean tea bag and passed the box back to his jailers, who kept it for him outside his cell, where it was not searched. Huntley carried out the elaborate scheme for two weeks, amassing what he judged would be a fatal dose. Before swallowing the tablets he wrote a suicide note. In it he said goodbye to Carr and requested that his brother, Wayne, should not be allowed to attend his funeral. After warders found him lying on the floor, he was taken to Milton Keynes General Hospital and given an urgent stomach pump. Doctors then placed him on a life-support machine and the next day he regained consciousness. He was immediately furious his plan had not succeeded, asking doctors: 'Why didn't you bastards let me die?' He later became more philosophical, saying his survival proved God did not want him dead. After 36 hours in the hospital, he was taken back to Woodhill.

This suicide attempt in the heart of one of the most secure jails in Britain sent shock waves through the whole Prison Service. The minister in charge of the service, Paul Goggins, made it the subject of an urgent report to Parliament. His comments on security at Woodhill were scathing; he said the prison had been 'complacent' and 'lax'. As Mr Goggins compiled his report, these failings were laid bare once again as the *News of the World* revealed that one of its reporters had got a job at Woodhill using a bogus CV and had been employed to watch over Huntley even though he was still undergoing training. David McGee had managed to take pictures of Huntley inside his cell, several of which were splashed across the newspaper on 15 June 2003. The shots showed an ill-shaven, puffy-faced Huntley wearing the jail's uniform burgundy sweatshirt and staring from his seat out of the window.

With the failings at Woodhill so graphically exposed, it was only a matter of time before Huntley was moved. Within weeks he would be on his way to Belmarsh Prison in south-east London, where again the authorities had constructed a cell for him. At a cost of £200,000, the prison had built a jail within a jail in the healthcare centre, using four cells and two other rooms. The suite was completely isolated from the rest of the prison, and Huntley was out of sight and earshot of any other inmate, his nearest neighbour being the Great Train Robber Ronnie Biggs, who was in a cell two floors above. Every surface in the block was smooth, so that Huntley had nowhere to hang a rope to kill himself. Here he would sit out the remaining time until his trial, spending his days using the PlayStation and gym provided for him and talking to anyone who would listen about Maxine Carr.

Although there were many who wanted Huntley and Carr killed, a huge amount of effort and taxpayers' money was to be expended in keeping them alive. From the moment Carr arrived at Holloway Prison on 21 August 2002, she was put in the segregation unit to separate her from the other inmates and protect her from possible attack. She was under round-the-clock observation, with warders checking her every 15 minutes and noting her condition in an orange book pinned to the wall outside her cell. In prison jargon this is what is known as a 20/52 self-harm monitoring book. In layman's terms, Carr was on suicide watch. The fragile-looking teaching assistant was classed as a Category A, or highest-risk, inmate and her cell was designed to thwart attempts at self-harm. The furniture, consisting of a table and chair, was made of cardboard. The walls and ceiling were moulded so that there were no projecting surfaces from which a ligature could be tied. Whatever the wishes of the Peterborough mob, Carr could not hang herself.

On her arrival at Holloway, Carr was in a fragile state; she had seen her world shattered, and despite all her efforts she had been separated from the man she totally depended on. Even at this early stage she knew their separation would probably last for life. Holloway, a grim brick structure with a reputation for violence and lesbian sexual abuse, was a forbidding prospect, and as Carr was led through the reception area on the first day of her incarceration she was staggering and in tears. She went through the admission procedures in a daze; she was given an overnight pack containing a toothbrush, soap and toothpaste, plus a pen and paper and a phone card to allow her to contact her family. She was seen by a doctor and given an outline of the regime by the officer in charge of her unit. She also received a visit from the chaplain. After that she was left in a state of almost total isolation.

Staff at the jail described Carr as being close to the edge during her first few weeks, crying herself to sleep every night. During the day she spent her time exercising compulsively, repeating an aerobics and stretching routine again and again. Warders noticed she seemed unable to keep still, despite being confined to her cell for much of the day. Under intense strain in the forbidding surroundings, she lost all interest in food and went for whole days without eating at all. The meals the warders brought to her cell were left untouched, and her anorexia returned with a vengeance.

In a letter sent to a friend on 6 September Carr wrote of her misery: 'Someone out there has hurt those two beautiful girls and they are laughing at the police and Ian and me. My probability of bail is good, only it would have to be a secure place with bodyguards or police watching out for me. At the moment, though, Holloway is probably the safest I'll get, outside I'd probably be killed. No wonder I can't eat and Ian's had a breakdown.' Prisoner GN9456 had been prescribed Valium and antidepressants in an attempt to calm her disturbed state. But by 19 October 2002 her normal eight-stone frame had shrunk dramatically, reaching just under six stone. Carr had been starving herself.

The full extent of her hunger strike became apparent that Saturday evening, when a warder carrying out another of the quarter-hourly checks on Carr's condition found her on the floor of her cell, unconscious. The lack of sustenance had finally sapped her energy to the point where her life was slipping away. Amid fears that she might not last the night, an ambulance was called and she was driven with a police escort to the Whittington Hospital, a mile away. Doctors there began to force-feed Carr via saline and glucose drips threaded through her nose. They found her a skeletal figure, with nurses saying she was 'no more than skin and bones'. But the high-energy fluid slowly brought her back to life.

Two days later she was judged well enough to return to Holloway, but she still steadfastly refused to eat and remained on a drip. Her plight reminded many of Moors Murderer Ian Brady, who at that point had not eaten solid food for three years. He was being kept alive against his wishes by liquid food pumped into him through a nose tube. However, Carr was to relent on her bid for self-starvation. As the weeks passed, and with the help of a psychotherapist, she began to accept food again and eventually returned to a normal diet. Even so, the hunger strike would not be Carr's last attempt at self-destruction in jail. On 25 May 2003 she tried to slash her wrists. But again she failed to cause serious damage, leaving only a shallow cut to her left wrist which did not pierce the artery.

In the weeks leading up to her hospitalisation Carr had continued a passionate correspondence with her fiancé. She sent the killer love letters at the rate of up to four a day, often staying awake late into the night scribbling notes to him in her spidery hand. Their tone was described as 'loving'. At times Carr discussed wedding plans. And in one emotional letter Huntley made Carr a renewed proposal of marriage. Another particularly passionate exchange saw them pledging to spend their lives together once they were freed, whenever that would be.

In a less optimistic vein, they also discussed suicide, with Huntley vowing to do away with himself. He told Carr his death would 'take the heat' off her, adding that he was having problems with his memory and he would be able to clear everything up once these were cured. Over the months following their arrest, scores of these letters passed between the couple. Huntley wrote to Carr every day, reserving the hours between 8pm and 1am for this purpose, then sleeping until 1pm.

By this point he was also receiving bundles of fan mail, mostly from women, every week. They would often enclose photographs of themselves and urge him to write back or telephone, and sometimes he would reply. In one reply the former caretaker wrote: 'Maxine is doing OK. Thank you. We write to each other regularly. I am writing to her again tomorrow. I got four letters from her today along with yours and some others.' The neat and precise handwriting, all in capital letters, conveyed an unmistakable strength of feeling. Locked up hundreds of miles apart, Huntley and Carr were still very much together.

Within two months of Carr trying to starve herself to death, a sudden change in her relationship with Huntley took place. With no warning, following a series of particularly warm love letters, she notified the authorities at Holloway that she would no longer accept correspondence from her fiancé. This apparently impulsive move on 10 December 2002 was the first sign that Carr was prepared to distance herself from the man who killed Holly and Jessica.

The effect on Huntley was devastating. A source at Woodhill said: 'When he was told he just went quiet and stared blankly ahead. He just said, "Yeah, yeah" as if it hadn't sunk in or he didn't believe it. The prison official had to ask him again if he really understood and he was shown Maxine's letter so he could see it was signed by her. He burst into tears.' Carr's request, addressed to Woodhill Governor Paul Mullen, said: 'I no longer wish to have any communication with Mr Ian Huntley.' Huntley had been cut off.

In the face of adversity Carr was finally beginning to act with her own interests at heart. If she remained tied to

Huntley, it was likely she would face a very lengthy jail term, and from behind bars he could not give her the support she so desperately needed. When Carr had appeared in court for the first time at Peterborough Magistrates' Court, she had been told she faced a possible life sentence. Since then she had been charged, at the Old Bailey on 17 January 2003, with two more counts of obstructing justice. This time prosecutors had spelt out their belief that she had known all along that Huntley had killed the girls. The charge sheet said: 'knowing or believing Ian Kevin Huntley had committed the said offence or some other arrestable offence ... [she] provided false accounts of her own whereabouts and the activities and whereabouts of Ian Kevin Huntley'. Carr's situation was desperate.

The effort to erase Huntley from her mind was enormous; still depressed and suicidal, she had to rid herself of the one pillar of support in her life. But she was not lacking in courage or the ability to suppress her emotions. She had shown both capabilities in ample degree while lying to the world about the killings of Holly and Jessica. Now she was to apply the same icy discipline to rejecting her boyfriend and repressing her feelings for him.

On 16 April 2003 she was to come face to face with Huntley for the first time since the couple had been arrested. The courts had decided that they should be tried together, side by side, at the Old Bailey. On this day they were to show up at the central London court for a pre-trial hearing where the judge would hear their pleas and make legal directions. Again the courtroom was packed with journalists. This time they were joined by Kevin and

Nicola Wells and Leslie and Sharon Chapman, who bravely decided they would witness the event.

The crowd in the Old Bailey's Court Number One huddled together in suspense, waiting for a glimpse of the two suspects. At 11.25am the door to the cells beneath banged open and Huntley walked up into the dock, surrounded by four prison guards. The sound of a hysterical woman screaming somewhere below drifted up through the open door and punctuated the quiet calm of the courtroom. The Wellses and Chapmans swivelled their eyes to get their first glimpse of the man accused of murdering their daughters. Seconds later Huntley was led out of court again – he had mistakenly been brought in before the judge had taken his seat. With Mr Justice Moses in place, he reappeared, followed by Carr. She had to take a deep breath as she walked up the steps and prepared to face the court.

It was then that the crowd were given a graphic display of Carr's determination to distance herself from her boyfriend. Huntley's eyes followed her as she climbed up to the dock, begging her to look back. But she ignored him completely. During the following 10-minute hearing, she did not glance once at the man who had been the subject of her devotion. Yet the couple sat only two feet apart. Huntley, on the other hand, seemed desperate to catch her eye, turning to face her four times in the hope that she would be looking back. But the pale, frail figure kept her head fixed forward.

The accused were made to stand in the dock as the charges were read. The Chapmans forced themselves to look at Huntley as the first charge – murdering their daughter Jessica – was read out. Not a flicker of emotion showed on Huntley's pasty face. He whispered almost inaudibly and stumbled over the words 'Not guilty'. The charge of murdering Holly Wells followed. This time it was her family's turn to stare. Once again there was no emotion on Huntley's face.

Carr closed her eyes, gulped and furrowed her brow before pleading not guilty, in a barely audible whisper, to plotting to pervert justice and helping an offender. On the fifth and joint charge of conspiracy to pervert justice, Huntley frowned before pleading guilty. As the hearing ended he stood forlornly in the dock and watched Carr again as she turned away from him and walked down the steps to the cells. He was left trying to snatch a glimpse of her through the mass of security guards.

At last it seemed the special bond between the two was broken, and the stage was set for a dramatic trial which would bring both to the justice they had tried so hard to escape.

18

THE TRIAL

Like everything else in the history of the Soham case, the trial was shaped by the devious, manipulative character of the murderer. From the moment he killed the girls, Huntley's excuses took on the qualities of a Russian doll – once one was cracked, underneath there lay another, equally well-formed shell of lies.

Now, cornered in the Old Bailey with an enormous weight of evidence against him, Huntley still tried to wriggle his way out of accepting full responsibility and punishment. Wheedling to the last, he concocted yet another tall story, claiming the girls' deaths had been a 'terrible accident'. He did not spare a thought for the families whose lives he had destroyed, shamelessly trying to rob them of that shred of comfort, the closure of seeing him and his girlfriend found guilty and sent to jail. The result of this reprehensible tactic was weeks of courtroom activity during which the wheels of justice rolled ponderously onwards at huge expense to the taxpaying public.

The scene was the Old Bailey's historic Number One court, and the two accused sat together once more in the dock before the gaze of the judge Mr Justice Moses and a jury of seven women and five men. Also in the room were the families of the murdered girls, Kevin and Nicola Wells, Sharon, Leslie, Rebecca and Alison Chapman, their faces bloodless and immobile under yet another ordeal. The benches at the back were crammed with dozens of members of the press from all over the world. The pale light of late Autumn filtered through the 68 glass panes of the domed ceiling above, down upon the two defendants, Huntley dressed in a shirt and tie and Carr equally formal in a grey suit.

In this solemn atmosphere on November 5, 2003, prosecutor Richard Latham QC opened his address at a slow, measured pace. He told of the girls' final walk, describing how the two friends wandered around their home town, then by pure chance fell into the hands of their killer. He pointed to a map of Soham on which their route was traced in red dots. He said Huntley had not been seen during a four-hour period on the night the girls went missing, and that the last signal from Jessica's mobile phone had been given off at 6.46pm from a small area which included the caretaker's house. Without changing the regular, precise rhythm of his speech, Mr Latham dropped a bombshell. He said, 'I now have a very significant piece of information. We understand that it is unlikely to be disputed that the two girls went into Huntley's home shortly after 6.30pm and that they died within a short time.' Kevin and Nicola whispered to each other. Leslie reached for a glass of water. The rest of the court was stunned into silence.

Mr Latham went on, describing how Huntley had changed his story on the night of the murders, telling one search party he had not seen the girls, then telling other people he had. Witnesses said his car was missing from its usual parking place earlier that night, and there were no lights on in the house. Mobile phone records and several witnesses had placed Carr in Grimsby when she said she was upstairs in the caretaker's cottage having a bath.

Mr Latham's words set the pattern for the prosecution case, a relentlessly detailed exposure of Huntley's guilt, and an overwhelmingly convincing account of how Carr had lied for him. Detectives had found 49 fibres from Holly and Jessica's Manchester United shirts in Huntley's house. His hairs were found in the bin along with the girls' burnt clothes. On the bag which had contained those clothes were his fingerprints. More fibres were found in the boot of Huntley's car, which also contained traces of soil and pollen of the types found in Common Drove. For all Huntley's attempts to wipe out the forensic traces of his crime, the sensitive instruments of modern science had got the better of him.

To help show how Holly and Jessica had met with their deaths, the members of the jury were driven to Soham to make their own inspection of Huntley's house. They retraced his steps across the floor of the dining room where he is thought to have killed the girls. Forensic experts had stripped the house completely; the bare rooms were distinguished from each other only by labels stuck to the walls. The jury was then taken to the desolate spot where Huntley dumped the bodies. Mr Latham guided them to the section of ditch where the girls were discovered. He said: 'And the bodies, therefore, were found just down here. Feel free to ...' his voice tailed off as he gestured towards the mud beneath.

Back in court, moving testimony was heard from the families of the girls. They told of the terrible night they had lost their daughters, of the desperate search into the early hours, and how Sharon and Nicola, in tears, had discussed which of them should call the police.

Sixteen days into the trial, defence counsel Stephen Coward QC revealed Huntley's latest and last string of excuses. Scheming away in his prison cell, he had pondered the details of the prosecution case which were disclosed to him in advance of the trial. He played crafty sick, claiming the trauma of his experiences had wiped his memory, and in the presence of police his mind simply seized up. In the early stages of the case prosecutors had little more than circumstantial evidence against him, and he hoped to deny having anything to do with the girls' deaths. He paved the way towards blaming someone else, telling his mother during a prison visit that a mysterious figure must have followed the girls after they left his house, murdered them then tried to frame him.

As detectives worked on the case, however, an increasing

amount of concrete evidence was uncovered. Huntley knew the girls could now be linked to his car and his house, and that officers could prove he had been at the spot where the bodies were dumped. Two weeks before the trial started, Huntley decided he had no choice but to admit he had killed Holly and Jessica. But he still had the glimmer of a chance. From prosecution papers, he could see that the one area of uncertainty was the exact chain of events inside 5 College Close. His repeated scrubbing of his house had achieved this much; there was no way of making certain where, when or how the girls were killed. And he was the only witness still alive.

So in Huntley's revised version of events, the double murder was caused not by his sick lust for children, but by Holly having a nosebleed. Because of this, she, Huntley and Jessica went up to the bathroom. The bath was full as Huntley had been washing the dog. Carrying some tissues to stem the flow of blood, he bumped into Holly, who was sitting on the edge of the bath. This glancing blow was enough to send the robust 10 year-old flying, hitting her head on the side of the tub and splashing into the water. According to Huntley, Jessica then screamed: 'You pushed her! You pushed her!' So he grabbed her by the mouth to shut her up. Not knowing his own strength, Huntley smothered the swimming champion and became aware that she was 'no longer supporting herself on her feet.' When he turned round Holly had spontaneously drowned in the bathwater. As Mr Coward came out with this tale, the crowds in the courtroom looked on in disbelief. Once more Huntley had managed to cast himself as the helpful caretaker trying to deal with an emergency, cruelly maligned and misunderstood.

Convinced he could hoodwink the system one last time, Huntley took the witness stand to explain his latest version of events. On oath in the highest court in the land, speaking before the parents of the girls he had killed, he wept false tears as he stumbled through another stream of lies. 'I wish I could turn back the clock,' he said. 'I wish I could do things differently. I wish none of this had ever happened. I'm sorry for what's happened and I'm ashamed of what I did. I accept that I'm responsible for the deaths of Holly and Jessica but there's nothing I can do about it now. I sincerely wish there was.' Huntley, wearing a dark grey suit and pale grey tie, sniffed repeatedly and appeared to be on the point of losing his composure. He sobbed out the words which resonated around the chamber, meeting with no response other than silence.

Huntley was guided through his 'accidental death' account by his lawyer Mr Coward. He had 'just panicked and froze' as Holly drowned and Jessica was somehow suffocated at his hands. He added, 'I checked Holly's breathing and her neck and wrist for a pulse. Up to that point I hadn't really been aware of Jessica. I hadn't registered that she was lying there. I put my face close to her mouth for breathing – I have never been really that hot at checking pulses. I sat in the corner on the landing just looking at Jessica. I had been sick. I knew I had to get the girls into my car and out of the house.'

Huntley told how he drove the bodies away and dumped

them in the ditch near Lakenheath. He said: 'I picked up one of the girls – I am not sure which one. The bank of the ditch was too steep to carry the girls down so I had to place one of them at the top of the ditch and push her so she rolled down and then returned to the car and did the same thing again.' He described pouring petrol over the bodies. 'I went part of the way down the ditch then backwards and forwards. The fire flared up.'

His motive in telling this tale had, he claimed, nothing to do with trying to get himself a lighter sentence. Instead he was doing his duty to the families of the two girls. He was so determined to accomplish this duty that he had even refrained from killing himself in prison. He said: 'I made my mum and dad a promise that I would get myself through to the trial so that Holly and Jessica's parents would hear what had happened.' So Kevin and Nicola Wells and Leslie and Sharon Chapman had to listen to Huntley speak about cutting off their daughters' clothes and burning them in a bin. The murderer said he then went home, smoked a few cigarettes and thought to himself: 'What have I done?'

Huntley's story contained a number of gaping flaws which were exposed in a masterful cross-examination by Mr Latham. If Holly had died in the bath, it could not have been an accident, because in normal circumstances either Huntley or Jessica would have rescued her. Jessica likewise could not have been accidentally smothered. If she had died in this manner she would have struggled for many seconds, and her death could only have been achieved by a determined, deliberate effort. Mr Latham made these points in a dramatic confrontation with the killer as follows:

> Mr Latham: If you had given that girl the
> slightest chance she would have lived,
> wouldn't she?
> Huntley: Yes.
> Mr Latham: You had killed her, hadn't you?
> Huntley: (*whispering*) Yes.
> Mr Latham: You advanced towards her.
> Huntley: Yes.
> Mr Latham: Putting up your hand towards her
> mouth?
> Huntley: Yes.
> Mr Latham: If you block the mouth and nose,
> what starts to happen to someone?
> Huntley: You starve them of oxygen.
> Mr Latham: They start, in effect, to die.
> Huntley: Yes.
> Mr Latham: It doesn't happen in a moment?
> Huntley: No.

Mr Latham asked Huntley to show how he put his hand over Jessica's mouth. Huntley raised his right hand and put it sideways across his mouth with the fingers near the nostrils. Mr Latham asked him what Jessica would have been doing if his hand was over her face and she could not breathe.

> Huntley: Struggling.

Mr Latham: Fighting for her very life, wouldn't she, Mr Huntley?

Huntley: Yes.

Mr Latham: The only way Holly could have drowned in the bath is if you were holding her under the water.

Huntley: I wasn't holding her.

Mr Latham: If Jessica was screaming it was because you were murdering Holly. That's the truth, isn't it?

Huntley: No.

Mr Latham: You watched Holly drown.

Huntley: I just froze, sir.

Mr Latham: Jessica would have pulled her friend's head out of the water. Effectively, the two of you stood within touching distance of this child and watched her drown?

Huntley: I didn't watch her drown. I comprehended that she was in the bath and she wasn't breathing. In these circumstances, it's easy to be rational. In those circumstances, it's not so rational. Believe me – I know.

Huntley had become increasingly rattled as Mr Latham drove holes through his story, and by now had raised his voice almost to a shout.

Mr Latham: You can be perfectly assertive when you want to, can't you?

Huntley: Yes.

Mr Latham: You can get angry, can't you,
Mr Huntley?
Huntley: Yes.
Mr Latham: You have just lost your temper
with me, haven't you?
Huntley: Yes.
Mr Latham: Did you lose your temper with one
of those girls? Did you become the assertive
individual you became two minutes ago?
Huntley: No, I didn't.

Huntley denied he had been driven by a sick sexual desire for the girls, and that he had found them 'too tempting'. He denied he intended to kill them. He said Carr, watching him from the dock a few feet away, had never known he had murdered Holly and Jessica. He added: 'I wanted to tell somebody. I tried on several occasions to tell Maxine but I couldn't get the words out. This is the first time that Maxine would have heard what happened that day.' Huntley claimed he told his girlfriend only that the girls had been in his house, and that they had walked away unharmed. He said Carr knew he had been accused of rape and that was why she decided to give him a false alibi. As he spoke, Carr looked on with her head bowed.

Despite her efforts to conceal his guilt, Huntley had finally admitted he killed the girls. It was a crushing moment for Carr, a moment when she realised, perhaps for the first time, the price she had paid for his evil acts. When she took the witness stand the next day, she, too, claimed Huntley's admission came as a revelation. Previously, she had been the dutiful girlfriend, now she was the wronged woman, whose only crime was to believe in the man she loved. Carr had come to the witness box publicly to turn her back on Huntley. It was her only chance to win over the court's sympathy.

Her lawyer Michael Hubbard QC asked Carr if she had loved Huntley. She replied: 'Very, very much, yes.' Did he appear to love her? 'I thought so,' she said. Her plans were 'hopefully, to get married when we were stable and working. I wanted children. He kept saying we'd have to wait.' Holly was 'the kind of daughter I would want to have.' Carr was a caring young woman who loved the girls and loved her boyfriend, who had not intentionally harmed anybody. Yet in Holloway prison she had been suffering terrible abuse – the inmates had dubbed her the new Myra Hindley.

Carr said Huntley begged her to lie for him. He wanted her to do so to 'anyone who asks'. She agreed for fear that the accusation of rape against him in 1998 would lead to him being framed. So, she admitted, she had lied to the police, to journalists and on TV. She said: 'Though I know it wasn't right in moral terms, I thought I was doing the right thing for that person. I didn't want Ian accused of anything that he hadn't done.'

Carr's determination to distance herself from Huntley drove her to a series of revelations which in effect constituted evidence against him. She described how she found the house on her return from Grimsby, the crack in the bath, the washing machine full of bedclothes and the strange flood in the dining room. She noticed he had swapped the carpet in the boot of the car. Seeing the clean-up, she suspected he had slept with another woman in the house. She admitted Huntley told her the girls had been inside their home, but claimed it did not cross her mind that the strange scenes had anything to do with them.

Carr, wearing a black polo-neck sweater and light blue jacket, defiantly stuck to her story as she was questioned by Huntley's lawyer Mr Coward. He wanted her to admit a more active role in concocting his alibi and concealing Huntley's guilt. Carr became increasingly emotional. She painted a picture of her relationship with Huntley, portraying him as a controlling, abusive figure who had 'pushed her into a corner' where she had not choice but to lie for him. The exchange continued as follows:

Mr Coward: You're making it up.
Carr: It's very embarrassing to be in a
relationship like this.
Mr Coward: You're making him out to be some
sort of domestic bad man when it wasn't true.
Carr: It's very, very, very true. I loved that man.
no matter what he did to me, I loved him.
Mr Coward: I suggest the simple truth is that
you were anxious to help.
Carr: No, sir, I was trying to make Ian look
better than he actually is. You have no idea
about the relationship I have with Mr Huntley.
I'm trying to make it clear the kind of person
Ian Huntley is towards me. I told a lie but I
was hardly going to tell the police that he is an

abusive person who controls you, because I was
scared – I was conscious I was going home to
that man at the end of the day.

Mr Coward again said Carr had embellished her story to put herself in a better light. It was then that she snapped. With tears of fury streaming down her cheeks, Carr jabbed her finger at Huntley and said: 'I know exactly what I have done, sir. I have come in this witness box and I am not going to be blamed for what that thing in that box has done to me or those children.'

Huntley, sitting 20 feet away in the dock, was stunned. He knew Carr had spurned him, but he was not prepared for this. His eyes were blank with despair, his face twisted into the expression of a wounded animal. Carr's rejection of him, he earlier told the court, had prompted his suicide attempt in jail. Now that rejection had turned into hatred. She was so full of venom that she could not bring herself to utter his name.

Carr was challenged again, this time by Mr Latham for the prosecution. He read to her the script of a TV interview in which she had repeated Huntley's alibi. Mr Latham said: 'You said, "I just wish I had been downstairs and had popped out and had a chat." That was your embellishment, wasn't it?'

The words moved Carr to tears for the second time during her testimony. Through her sobs she replied: 'I have been feeling very guilty, sir, for a long, long time that if I was there I could have stopped them from dying. But yes, I lied.'

Carr insisted she had not known the girls were dead. She had cleaned up after the murders not because she had conspired with Huntley but because she was 'obsessive' about tidiness. She had referred to the girls in the past tense in interviews merely because she had worked with them in the past. She had cried over the car boot because she was upset about Holly and Jessica disappearing, not because she knew Huntley had used it to transport their bodies.

Carr's defence lawyer Mr Hubbard asked to re-examine his client to clarify an important point. It was, he suggested, implausible that she would have continued to have sex with Huntley knowing he had killed two children.

> Mr Hubbard: Did you sleep in the same bed as Ian Huntley that night?
> Carr: Yes.
> Mr Hubbard: And on the days up to your eventual arrest?
> Carr: Yes.
> Mr Hubbard: Would you have been in the same bed if you believed for a moment that he had unlawfully killed those two children?
> Carr: I wouldn't be in the same house as him.

And so the Soham murder case ended very much as it had begun, with the two suspects protesting their purity. Mr Latham in his closing speech described the pair as 'accomplished liars'. Examining Huntley's story, he said: 'We invite you to reject the accounts of both deaths as desperate lies, the only way out for him. We suggest that this whole business in the house was motivated by something sexual. But whatever he initiated plainly went wrong. Thereafter, in this ruthless man's mind, both girls had to die in his own selfish self-interest. Each was a witness, a potential complainant, and he was quite merciless.' Turning to Carr, Mr Latham added: 'She had the prospect of marriage, a baby, a nice home and a new start. She preferred to do what she could to make the best of the position she was in. That involved at all costs protecting Ian Huntley.'

In the event, the jury was to accept almost all of Mr Latham's case. On Wednesday December 17 2003, after four days of deliberation, they had reached their verdicts. The court was filled with an expectant silence as everyone waited to hear the crucial decision. Huntley and Carr in the dock, Kevin and Nicola Wells, Leslie, Sharon and Rebecca Chapman a few feet away, the massed ranks of the media at the back of the courtroom – all were on knife's edge of suspense. How did they find the defendant Ian Kevin Huntley? Guilty of the murder of Jessica Chapman. Guilty of the murder of Holly Wells. Holly's mother Nicola burst into tears; her father Kevin smiled with relief. Carr was guilty of plotting a fake alibi with her boyfriend. She was not guilty of helping a man she knew or believed was the killer.

Mr Justice Moses ordered Huntley to stand up. He said: 'Ian Kevin Huntley, on 4 August 2002, you enticed two 10-year-old girls, Holly Wells and Jessica Chapman, into your house. They were happy, intelligent and loyal. They were much loved by their families and all who knew them. You murdered them both. You are the one person who knows how you murdered them. You are the one person who knows why. You destroyed the evidence. But you showed no mercy and you show no regret. It is plain that once you killed one you had to kill the other in your attempt to avoid detection.

'On 10 August you told the BBC that you thought you might be the last friendly face that these girls had to speak to. That was a lie which serves to underline the persistent cruelty of your actions. On the contrary, one of these girls died knowing her friend had been attacked or killed by you. After you had murdered them both, you pushed their bodies into a ditch, stripped them and burned them while their families searched for them in increasing despair. And as Kevin Wells called out their names, you pretended to join in the search. Three days later, you demonstrated the extent of your merciless cynicism by offering that father some words of regret.

'Your tears have never been for them, only for yourself. In your attempts to escape responsibility, in your lies and your manipulation up to this day, you have increased the suffering you have caused two families. There is no greater task for the criminal justice system than to protect the vulnerable. There are few worse crimes than your murder of those two young girls.'

The judge gave Huntley a life sentence for each murder. This time there was no escape; no lies, no feigned madness could save him now. With his guilt finally exposed for all to see, there was no point putting on a show of emotion and not a flicker of feeling passed over his face. As the killer was led down from the dock to the cells beneath, Jessica's sister Rebecca waved him goodbye and good riddance.

Carr was sentenced to three-and-a-half years for her part in covering up the murders. Mr Justice Moses told her, 'Your selfish concern for yourself and Huntley led you to lie all too readily and glibly. If you had the slightest regard for those girls or their families you would have told the truth.'

Minutes later Holly and Jessica's brave parents were facing the world's media to speak of their relief at seeing justice done. Kevin Wells said the families had feared right up to the last moment that Huntley's lies would hoodwink the jury. His wife Nicola was still in tears. Leslie Chapman told of his contempt for the man who had ruined all their lives. He said, 'I think he was a time bomb waiting to go off and both our girls were in the wrong place at the wrong time. I hope the next time I see him will be like we saw our daughters – and it will be in a coffin.'

Leslie's wish that Huntley will die in jail may well come true. As he spoke, the killer was in the back of a prison van, heading off to begin what is likely to be a lifetime behind bars.

THE AFTERMATH

Like With Huntley and Carr consigned to jail, Holly's and Jessica's parents were granted that scrap of solace that comes with knowing justice has been done. They could have been forgiven for hoping the conclusion of the court case would be the last they would ever hear of the killer or his protector. Sadly, the expectation that Huntley and Carr would finally keep quiet and accept their punishment was not to be fulfilled: instead of taking what they deserved and allowing the Wellses and the Chapmans to get on with coping with their grief, the pair continued to work their way through the justice system, always with the aim of gaining the greatest advantage.

The tactics used by Huntley and Carr were strikingly similar, but there were important differences. Carr, sent to jail for the lesser offence, had the opportunity to use the legal system to further her cause. She would make full use of every available legal means, forcing through measures to ensure her comfort, some of which would become landmarks in British law. Huntley, who was left with fewer options following his conviction for double child murder, would nevertheless pursue a campaign for leniency through the media. For both of them, the objectives were the same: the pair who had brought so much pain to innocent people were determined to get the best out of the system that they possibly could.

In her defence at the Old Bailey, Carr had presented herself as Huntley's victim. She succeeded to the extent that she convinced the jury she had not known that her boyfriend had murdered the girls. Her defence involved the publicly perceived very sudden dropping of all affection for him, the public renunciation of all ties and the increasing insistence that she herself had been manipulated. She presented herself as the wronged woman, the innocent who had merely tried to cover up his true movements as an act of loyalty. Her only crime, she suggested, had been an excess of love.

In the aftermath of her imprisonment, it became the orthodox view in some quarters that Carr was indeed a wronged woman, although readers of this book will realise that the reality was not so straightforward. Her response to being given a three and a half year sentence was immediately to try to reduce it and make it less arduous in every manner possible. She convinced the authorities at Holloway Prison that she was a special case, a particularly vulnerable young person who deserved a transfer to the much more sympathetic Foston Hall in Derbyshire. The prison is far softer than Holloway: according to the *Prisons Handbook*, 'There are extensive grounds and good opportunities for access to fresh air.'

Ever quick to spot an opportunity, Carr also realised that her relatively short prison sentence made her eligible for release under the electronic tagging scheme recently introduced by the then home secretary, David Blunkett. Unfortunately for Carr, her bid for early freedom was rumbled by the newspapers. The public was outraged, the feeling being that she should pay her debt to society by serving her full term of imprisonment. Anger spilled over into criticism of Blunkett's tagging scheme, and the rules were changed overnight to block Carr's release and so stem the inevitable political backlash that would have resulted. The home secretary, it suddenly emerged, was empowered to prevent a tagging going ahead in cases of notorious prisoners whose release could bring his scheme into disrepute. This ruling was tantamount to admitting that Carr's release was being blocked to prevent adverse publicity.

As Carr served out the last weeks of her sentence in relative comfort, plans were being drawn up to make sure she remained comfortable after her release. She would be given a new identity, her appearance would be changed with the help of experts, she would live in a secret location and be guarded by the police. Large amounts of taxpayers' money would be spent safeguarding her from vigilante attacks. Carr's lawyers applied for a High Court injunction that would ban the press from revealing her new identity, or from indicating where she lived. This application was granted, and a draconian order was issued which forbade journalists from even so much as trying to find out where Carr was, or what she was doing. Carr's safety, it seemed, was worth any price. Any amount of public money would be spent to ensure it, and any democratic right – such as freedom of speech – would be sacrificed.

The move to protect Carr was just one of a series of legal and political developments that followed the Soham case. As the murders of Holly and Jessica continued to gather worldwide notoriety, a public inquiry was set up into how Huntley was allowed to get close to them in the first place. The Bichard Inquiry examined why Huntley was permitted to work as a school caretaker despite his long history of sex crimes. Thousands of pounds were spent pondering this question, which had a simple and obvious answer: Huntley was not identified as a risk to children because he had never been convicted and so did not have a criminal record. The fact that a serial sex offender managed to continue his crime spree across 10 years of his life of course represents a failure in policing. He was very obviously guilty of having underage sex with the 15-year-old mother of his child. In addition, at least one charge of rape, and a charge of burglary were inexplicably ordered to lie on file. The question remains as to why Huntley wasn't brought to trial long before he moved to Soham. Holly and Jessica lost their lives because a sex offender was somehow allowed to get away with so much for so long. Huntley got what he wanted by using lies and violence. He came to believe that he could get away with murder too.

The Bichard Inquiry, however, focussed on possible

weaknesses in the police computer system. The inquiry recommended a shake-up in the police database on criminals, suggesting that in future even those cleared of crimes ought to have records against their names. The concept of such a comprehensive database held the danger that false accusations against innocent people could be stored by the police and used in vetting processes of the kind Huntley had passed. The upshot of the inquiry was the potential erosion of another democratic right, that of being presumed innocent of a crime until proven guilty in court.

While the Bichard Inquiry rumbled on, minor details remained to be cleared up in the handling of Carr. Police discovered she had lied repeatedly to defraud the public purse of £4,000 in state benefits. She was convicted on 15 counts of fraud at Nottingham Crown Court, having falsely stated that she was living on her own in order to obtain housing benefit when she was actually living with Huntley. Carr had also made up GCSE and A-level results to get jobs, which included the teaching assistant post at St Andrew's Primary School in Soham. Facing a court once more on these charges, she again claimed all the lies were down to Huntley's domination, and escaped without adding to her prison sentence. The court could have jailed her for up to 10 years for these offences.

Carr walked free from prison in May 2004 having served just one year and nine months for providing Huntley with an alibi. Considering she had impeded one of the largest child-murder investigations in British history, she had got herself into a comfortable position very quickly. She would be protected by anonymity and, if necessary, police guards for the rest of her life.

Circumstances were a little harder for Huntley. His prospects for early release seemed very remote, but that did not deflect his determination never to give up, never to admit culpability or accept his punishment. He would carry on using the system to the very end because he knew from experience how well this worked. Huntley wanted better treatment in jail, a move to an easier prison, more privileges, and to be less detested by fellow inmates. His completely guilt-free mind craved the possibility, however distant, of release. If that was never to be achievable, he wanted the opportunity to commit suicide. Among all these wants, he also craved money – money to pay for prison perks and to provide for his parents who found themselves unemployable as a result of his crime.

Huntley approached the author in March 2004. He wanted to communicate using his parents, Kevin and Lynda, as go-betweens. In a series of conversations, they outlined Huntley's plan. He would sell his story for use in a new edition of this book, guaranteeing that what he said would be his first truthful account of the Soham murders. He said that he had lied in court and the version of events put forward at the Old Bailey had been pure fabrication.

Unsurprisingly, his new version proved equally implausible as the fabrications he told the jury at his trial. However, it offered some telling insights into his thought processes. Essentially it was a piece of propaganda, the intention of which was to diminish Huntley's status as a figure of hate. He had recently been reminded of just how much he was hated in Belmarsh Prison when a burglar, Freddie Asher, walked up to him in the corridor just outside his cell and, without warning, thumped him in the face. As Huntley saw it, such treatment was caused by the unjust amount of public disgust thrown in his direction. The Soham murders, he complained, had only received such massive attention because they took place in August, in the middle of the summer holiday season when there were few other stories for the press to concern themselves with. The whole thing had been blown out of proportion because the story had been kept running in the newspapers for two weeks.

That, he believed, was Carr's fault. She had told him to brazen out the manhunt when he had wanted to give himself up straight away. People were upset with him because he burned the girls' bodies, but Carr had ordered him to do that. Everyone was completely wrong in believing he was motivated by the twisted lust of a paedophile. He had been labelled a 'nonce' – or child molester – in jail, and that was totally unfair. Holly's death had been an innocent accident. True, he had murdered Jessica deliberately, but only to protect himself from the police.

This amazing string of excuses was passed to the author through Huntley's parents. Once again the killer was using every possible strategy to absolve himself of blame and avoid the uncomfortable consequences of his actions. Furious at being outflanked by Carr's courtroom betrayal, he wanted to wreak revenge on her, implicating her in the events at Soham as much as possible. Transferring some of the blame to her would, he hoped, reduce his own responsibility and improve his conditions. She had, he believed, got off lightly. Pretending to confess, apparently with no motive other than an impulse of honesty, would hoodwink people into believing he was not a paedophile. The story was cunningly constructed, and so utterly typical of Huntley.

The murderer's parents clearly believed his new account. Both had been driven to despair by their son's crimes. Lynda had suffered a mini-stroke and Kevin had sunk into depression. Things were so desperate, Kevin said, that neither of them could ever smile in public. Just a flicker of happiness would be enough to provoke a vigilante attack, and Kevin had already received beatings. The couple had even considered driving together off the cliffs at Scarborough on the Yorkshire coast to end their misery. They said their son was also on the brink of suicide, and would without doubt kill himself given the slightest opportunity.

In a meeting at a pub in Lincolnshire, Kevin and Lynda explained they had no choice but to support their son. When speaking to me on his behalf, they had no choice but to follow his wishes. Although they were not interested in money, Huntley insisted his new story would appear in print and he would be paid for telling it. They said they had already received thousands of pounds on his behalf for information given to newspapers. Some of that money, they said, had been used to buy Huntley treats to make his life in prison less unpleasant.

Huntley's offer this time was to confess to the author in

person behind the bars of Wakefield high-security prison in West Yorkshire. Huntley wanted to spin out a confession to make himself look better, and even wanted to be paid for his trouble. The sickening proposal was a perfect expression of a character who believed he had a right to everything but the responsibility for nothing. Of course, the author did not pay Huntley or anyone associated with him. His confession was eventually published by a newspaper and immediately dismissed by detectives as a fantasy. On the basis of large amounts of evidence, they believe Huntley is a paedophile and serial rapist who murdered the girls because he was motivated by a perverted lust and a desire to conceal those cravings. They believe he killed both girls deliberately. The nearest we can get to a true and complete account of how Huntley killed the girls remains the train of events described in these pages.

At the time of writing, Huntley is still locked up in Wakefield Prison. Huntley continues to do anything to avoid facing the consequences of his actions. His behaviour is a continuing disgrace, and the fact that aspects of it are tolerated and even financed is perhaps even more of a disgrace. However, for all their despicable twisting and turning, Huntley and Carr will, in reality, never be able to shake off the consequences of their crimes. No number of bogus stories or undeserved protection from the state will alter the scorn people feel for these two. Their actions, recorded in this book, will follow both of them wherever they go, for as long as they live.